MAKING WORK EASIER WITH MODERN AI TOOLS: A PRACTICAL GUIDE FOR SMALL TEAMS

Abhilash Pakalapati

Xoffencer

www.xoffencerpublication.in

ISBN-13: 978-93-47006-62-3 (Paperback)

Publication Date: 12 March 2026

MRP: ₹ 1500/-

ISBN

9 789347 006623

Published by:

Xoffencer International Book Publication House

Admin Office: *838/27, Behind Shyam Vihar Vatika, Laxmi Colony*
Dabra, Gwalior, Madhya Pradesh, India – 475110

London Office: *Suite RA01, 195-197 Wood Street*
London, United Kingdom, E17 3NU

www.xoffencerpublication.in
admin@xoffencerpublication.in, info@xoffencerpublication.in

Co-Powered by XOFFENCER GROUP

Research Partner

Featured

Credit: ***Cover Designed by: Satyam soni***
Content Formatting: Anjali Bhadoriya

Online Selling Partner

amazon

Flipkart

Google Play Books

doi

Author Details

Abhilash Pakalapati

Senior Data Engineer
Fannie Mae, Reston, Virginia, United States

Abhilash Pakalapati is a Senior Data Engineer and Generative AI practitioner with over a decade of experience transforming complex data and manual processes into simple, scalable, AI-driven systems. He specializes in modern cloud data architectures, RAG and LLM applications, and MLOps automation, helping organizations turn raw data into practical business value. Across banking, retail, and industrial domains, Abhilash has built production-ready analytics and AI platforms that enable teams to move from fragmented reporting to automated, insight-driven decision-making. A Fellow of the Soft Computing Research Society and a Databricks Lakehouse certified professional, he is known for translating advanced technologies into usable workflows for small and mid-sized teams. Through his work, Abhilash focuses on making modern AI tools approachable, efficient, and genuinely time-saving for everyday business use.

Preface

The text has been written in simple language and style in well organized and systematic way and utmost care has been taken to cover the entire prescribed procedures for Science Students.

We express our sincere gratitude to the authors not only for their effort in preparing the procedures for the present volume, but also their patience in waiting to see their work in print. Finally, we are also thankful to our publishers **Xoffencer Publishers, Gwalior, Madhya Pradesh** for taking all the efforts in bringing out this volume in short span time.

Contents

CHAPTER 1

THE NEW LANDSCAPE OF PRACTICAL AI

1.1 AI BEYOND BIG ENTERPRISES

Artificial intelligence was long thought to be a luxury that only big businesses and highly regarded research institutes could afford. The concept of employing AI was strongly associated with large financial outlays, intricate infrastructure, and groups of highly skilled experts. Smaller businesses frequently thought AI was beyond their price range. They linked it to costly servers, protracted development periods, and technological dangers that were out of their price range. As a result, AI stayed out of the mainstream, particularly in small firms, educational institutions, and tiny technical teams.

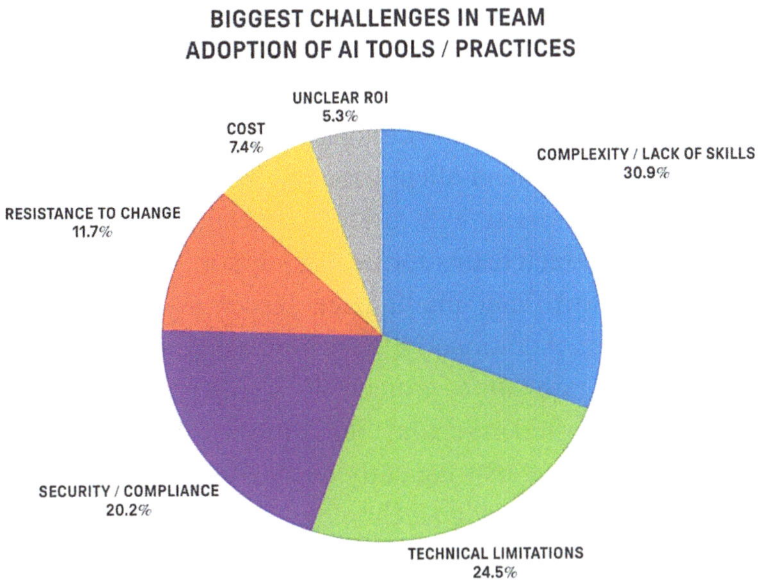

Figure 1.1: Adoption of modern AI tools by small teams and non-enterprise users.

In the early days of AI development, this view was not wholly incorrect. Large datasets, custom-built models, and on-going technical support were necessary for traditional AI systems. Strong financial support was necessary for organizations to try new things, fail, and get better. The price of admission alone deterred exploration for smaller firms. Adoption of AI was impractical due to implementation issues, even in cases where enthusiasm existed. The landscape of technology started to shift throughout time. The delivery and consumption of AI have changed significantly as a result of cloud computing advancements. Organizations can now acquire AI capabilities through cloud-based platforms rather than creating systems from the ground up. By taking care of processing, storage, and updates, these platforms free users to concentrate on results rather than infrastructure. AI tools are becoming easier to use and more intuitive due to advancements in software design.

AI is no longer limited to big businesses nowadays. Simple interfaces and subscription-based models make it accessible to lean tech teams, small businesses, and educational institutions. Numerous tools are reasonably priced, and some even provide free basic access. Smaller businesses can now experiment with AI without taking significant financial risks thanks to this change. The fact that contemporary AI products are made for non-technical users is among the biggest shifts. Deep programming knowledge is no longer necessary for people to take advantage of AI. With little training, small teams can automate regular documentation, teachers can create lesson plans, and business owners may analyze customer feedback. The emphasis is now on using AI rather than creating it.

The effects of this change are seen in many industries. AI is used by small organizations to manage communication, comprehend client behavior, and optimize processes. AI is used by educational institutions to assist with performance monitoring, grading, and lesson planning. AI is used by small tech teams for testing support, coding help, and requirement analysis. In each instance, artificial intelligence serves as a useful tool rather than a sophisticated research system. Additionally, AI is now a component of everyday processes rather than a stand-alone innovation project. It is integrated into current tools and procedures rather than being tested in separate initiatives. AI feels approachable and natural as a result of its integration. Workers frequently engage with AI as part of their daily work without considering it to be cutting-edge technology.

Key reasons why AI has moved beyond big enterprises include:

- Cloud-based delivery that removes infrastructure requirements
- Affordable pricing models suitable for small organizations
- User-friendly interfaces designed for everyday users
- Faster deployment without long implementation cycles

The change in perspective is another crucial element. Businesses are now more concerned with how to employ AI to increase productivity than with whether they can create it. The adoption of AI is now more pragmatic and goal-oriented as a result of this shift in perspective. Organizations concentrate on resolving particular issues rather than promoting innovation in and of itself. The introduction of AI into daily tasks has also altered productivity standards. Things that used to take hours of hard labor can now be finished in a matter of minutes. While repetitive workload is decreased, human engagement is still necessary.

AI aids in execution, but humans are still in charge of judgment and decision-making. The democratization of technology is reflected in the expansion of AI beyond large corporations. Budget and size are no longer barriers to access. Clarity of purpose and adaptability are becoming more important. AI can help businesses of any size as long as they know what they need and start small. AI's contribution to daily tasks will only grow as it develops further. The gap between cutting-edge technology and day-to-day operations has greatly reduced. Large organizations are no longer the exclusive owners of AI. It is now a useful tool that facilitates actual work in a variety of fields, sizes, and skill levels.

1.2 WHAT PRACTICAL AI REALLY MEANS

Practical AI is not about complex algorithms, advanced mathematics, or futuristic promises. It is about useful application. At its core, practical AI refers to the use of artificial intelligence to solve real, everyday problems that people face in their work environments. The emphasis is not on how AI models are created, but on what they help users achieve in a reliable and efficient way. For many users, AI becomes meaningful only when it directly improves daily tasks. Practical AI focuses on outcomes such as saving time, reducing manual effort, improving accuracy, and maintaining consistency. It is designed to fit naturally into existing workflows rather than forcing users to change the way they work.

Practical AI as a Tool for Everyday Work

Instead of being a technical experiment, AI serves as a support system in real-world situations. Most professionals don't need to know how neural networks work or how AI is trained. Whether AI can assist them in doing tasks more effectively is what counts. Repetitive and time-consuming tasks like reading a lot of material, summarizing data, creating documents, answering questions, or organizing content are frequently part of daily job. Because it can perform these repetitive jobs without continual supervision, practical AI is valuable. Practical AI enhances human thought rather than replaces it. AI manages tasks that need a lot of execution, while humans are still in charge of judgment, creativity, and decision-making. Teams and individuals can concentrate on higher-value tasks that call for knowledge and experience thanks to this balance.

Simplicity and Accessibility in Practical AI

Accessibility is one of the characteristics that distinguish practical AI. Modern useful AI tools are made for non-technical users, in contrast to previous AI systems that needed specialized infrastructure and technical know-how. Simple interfaces like file upload, dashboards, and text prompts are how they work.

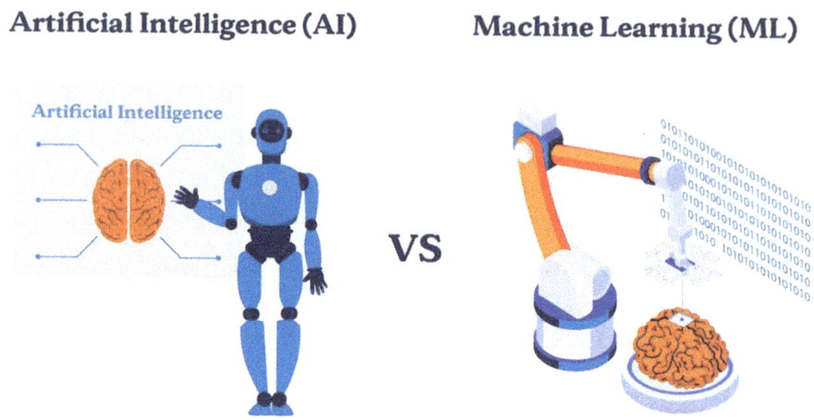

Figure 1.2: AI functioning as a daily productivity tool rather than a research technology.

Since these solutions are frequently cloud-based, complicated setup or local installation are not necessary. AI may be used by anyone with no expertise, and a lot of applications are inexpensive or provide free trial access. Because of its accessibility, practical AI can be used by small businesses, academic institutions, and small teams without specialized technical departments. Additionally, useful AI technologies are designed to seamlessly interface with pre-existing applications. Whether its spreadsheets, documents, emails, or project management systems, AI can be added as an enhancement rather than a replacement. This ease of integration reduces resistance and encourages adoption.

Where Practical AI Creates Real Value

When practical AI is constantly used for everyday tasks, its true worth becomes apparent. When made on a daily basis, even minor adjustments can eventually result in large increases in productivity. With AI assistance, tasks that once required hours may frequently be finished in minutes. When work follows a predictable pattern, practical AI works very well. For instance, AI is dependable when it comes to organizing information, creating standard reports, evaluating structured data, and creating periodic documents. By doing these activities, AI lessens human tiredness and the possibility of repetition-related errors.

In practical use, AI typically supports work in the following ways:

- Automating repetitive and rule-based tasks
- Assisting with data-heavy analysis and summarization
- Generating drafts and structured outputs for review
- Improving consistency across similar tasks

These contributions do not require AI to be perfect. Instead, they require AI to be dependable and easy to guide.

Measurable Impact over Theoretical Innovation

Results, not innovation, are used to evaluate practical AI. Measurable gains like faster turnaround times, fewer mistake rates, and more consistency are used to gauge its effectiveness. Practical AI does not seek to exhibit technical expertise, in contrast to experimental AI programs. It seeks to provide measurable and observable benefit. Businesses implementing useful AI frequently begin modestly. They use AI to streamline a single task that takes up needless time. The use of AI steadily grows once the advantages become apparent. This method prevents irrational expectations while fostering trust. Instead of innovation for its own sake, the emphasis is still on quantifiable improvements in day-to-day tasks. When practical AI is integrated into everyday tasks rather than being a stand-alone or specialized endeavor, it thrives.

Practical AI as a Long-Term Work Partner

Practical AI develops over time from a useful tool to a trustworthy collaborator. AI outputs become more in line with actual requirements as users improve workflows and instructions. This steady progress boosts self-esteem and promotes broader adoption. Practical AI's ability to scale support without adding to workload is what gives it long-term value. AI manages more execution tasks without getting tired as the number of labor increases. Humans continue to be in charge, evaluating results and reaching final judgments. Artificial intelligence does not negate the necessity of human intervention. Rather, it changes the balance of labor between humans and robots. When applied carefully, it produces a long-lasting model in which efficiency rises without sacrificing accountability or quality.

Practical AI is essentially the application of AI where it is most needed, namely in the routine tasks that constitute actual labor. It is about utility rather than complication. It's about impact, not experimentation.

1.3 EVERYDAY PROBLEMS AI CAN SOLVE

Regardless of their size or industry, modern firms deal with a similar set of operating difficulties. Employees frequently dedicate a sizable amount of their working hours to monotonous but essential tasks. Time and mental effort are required for documentation, data evaluation, report creation, internal communication, and basic analysis. Even though these duties keep businesses operating, they hardly ever directly support innovation, expansion, or strategic thinking. Because of this, competent workers are often busy but not very productive. Practical AI joins this market as a support system that effectively manages repetitive tasks rather than as a substitute for human labor. AI frees humans to concentrate on judgment, creativity, and higher-value decision-making by taking over monotonous and structured activities. Understanding the everyday problems AI can solve is essential to using it effectively.

Time-Consuming Routine Work in Organizations

Spending too much time on mundane tasks is one of the most prevalent issues in day-to-day employment. Workers in different departments deal with daily tasks that follow similar patterns. Although they are all necessary, writing reports, updating papers, analyzing emails, gathering data, and summarizing information seldom ever call for careful consideration. Documentation alone takes up hours each week in many organizations. Manual writing, frequent formatting, and revisions are all part of the process. Another challenge is data review. Before significant analysis can even start, staff members must examine spread sheets, find errors, verify completeness, and extract fundamental insights. These procedures are intellectually taxing and slow, which over time raises the possibility of errors.

An additional layer of work is added via communication. While they require attention, drafting emails, creating updates for stakeholders, and answering standard inquiries don't provide much creative fulfillment. This continuous involvement in low-value work eventually lowers motivation and productivity. In order to overcome these obstacles, practical AI automates the most tedious aspects of daily tasks. It can quickly read vast amounts of text, condense important ideas, and produce well-organized drafts. Employees are given pre-made outputs that just need to be reviewed and improved upon rather than having to start from scratch. The time spent on basic execution is greatly decreased by this change.

AI is particularly effective in areas such as:

- Summarizing long documents or meeting notes into concise formats
- Organizing unstructured data into readable and usable forms

By handling these foundational tasks, AI helps organizations move faster without increasing pressure on their workforce.

Reducing Cognitive Load and Improving Focus

Cognitive overload is another significant everyday issue that AI helps to resolve. Context switching is essential in today's workplaces. An employee may progress from data analysis to email response, report preparation, and finally meeting attendance. Frequent switching impairs output quality and concentration. This issue is also exacerbated by simple analysis jobs. Workers frequently carry out basic computations, comparisons, and pattern identification by hand. Despite their simplicity, these jobs demand constant focus. Mental exhaustion eventually sets in, resulting in slower productivity and more mistakes. Through the replacement of tasks with well-defined patterns, practical AI lessens cognitive stress. Without human assistance, it is able to examine statistics, identify trends, and expose anomalies.

Humans are still involved in the process, but their function has altered. Employees assess insights that have already been prepared for them rather than looking for information .For instance, a team can utilize AI to arrange and condense the data rather than going over hundreds of entries by hand. Then, human labor is used where it is most needed: in decision-making and result interpretation. Instead of causing continuous mental strain, this method helps people work more clearly and with greater focus. By providing information in an organized and comprehensible manner, AI also aids in decision-making. Decisions are made more quickly and confidently when the information is clear. Better results and more efficient workflows follow over time.

Daily Efficiency Gains That Compound over Time

The cumulative impact of practical AI is one of its most potent features. AI's advantages are not always immediately apparent. Rather, they manifest as daily repetitions of tiny, steady advancements. At first glance, it might not seem like much to save 10 minutes on a report, fifteen minutes on data preparation, or a few minutes on each email. The results, however, become significant when these minor savings spread across teams and over the course of weeks and months. Workers recover time that could be used for planning, education, teamwork, or creativity. Businesses benefit from increased uniformity, quicker turnaround times, and greater utilization of human resources. Routine chores are always completed in the same manner thanks to practical AI. Confusion and rework are decreased by this consistency. Workers no longer have to worry about missing steps or reinventing processes. Workflows with AI help give everyday operations predictability and dependability.

Reduced human weariness is another significant benefit. Repeated work reduces engagement and depletes mental energy. Employees are more focused and feel less burdened when AI manages routine execution. Job happiness and productivity both increase as a result. When businesses begin incorporating AI into regular processes rather than viewing it as a one-time tool, the actual benefits of the technology become apparent. AI becomes a silent productivity partner when it is applied regularly to repetitive tasks. Businesses that carefully implement useful AI eventually obtain a competitive edge through increased productivity, sharper concentration, and more intelligent use of human labor. Though technology doesn't cure every issue, practical AI tackles the most prevalent ones that subtly reduce productivity on a daily basis. AI helps businesses work smarter without working harder by managing repetitive tasks effectively, lowering cognitive load, and producing little but consistent efficiency benefits.

1.4 TYPES OF AI TOOLS USED IN DAILY WORK

Artificial intelligence is now a useful component of daily work, transcending sophisticated enterprise systems and experimental labs. Data scientists and engineers are no longer the exclusive users of modern AI systems. Teachers, office workers, analysts, supervisors, and small teams that prioritize outcomes above technical complexity can use them directly. Organizations now approach everyday chores, productivity, and decision-making differently as a result of this transition.

The majority of contemporary AI technologies function via web-based systems with straightforward, intuitive user interfaces. Instead of writing code, users engage with these tools through the use of natural language, uploaded files, or pre-made templates. Because of its accessibility, AI can be beneficial to non-technical individuals without requiring a lot of training. Therefore, rather of being viewed as a distinct or specialized system, AI is becoming more and more integrated into everyday activities.

AI Tools for Analysis and Decision Support

Analysis and decision support are the main areas of attention for one significant category of AI solutions. These technologies assist users in making sense of vast amounts of data that would be challenging to handle manually otherwise. People frequently have to review documents, datasets, feedback, or reports under time pressure in their regular work situations. By swiftly processing data and presenting it in an organized manner, analytical AI technologies lessen this load. AI-powered analytical tools, for instance, may discover trends in datasets, summarize lengthy documents, and extract important information from reports. These techniques can identify recurrent themes in survey-based enterprises by scanning thousands of responses. Educational institutions, they are able to determine learning gaps by analyzing data on student performance.

They can evaluate emails, policy documents, and meeting notes in offices and provide succinct summaries. Human judgment is not replaced by these tools. Rather, they help it by lessening cognitive strain. While AI takes care of the labor-intensive data processing, humans are still in charge of interpretation and decision-making. Everyday tasks are completed more quickly and accurately thanks to this division of labor. Pattern recognition is a key feature of analytical AI technologies. Humans are adept at comprehending context, but they have trouble identifying patterns in vast amounts of data. In these cases, AI shines. Similarities, irregularities, and patterns that might not be immediately apparent can be found using it. Because of this, analytical AI is especially useful in jobs involving quality assurance, performance monitoring, and feedback analysis.

AI Tools for Content Creation and Workflow Automation

Workflow automation and content production are the main areas of attention for a second significant category of AI technologies. Because they drastically cut down on the amount of time spent on repetitive tasks, these technologies are frequently employed in daily work. AI technologies for content creation help users with lesson planning, report drafting, presentation preparation, documentation writing, and the production of structured text for communication. Preparing written content takes up a large amount of time in professional settings. While necessary, emails, reports, proposals, and directions are monotonous. AI tools assist by using user input to generate preliminary drafts. Users may concentrate on improving material rather than beginning from scratch because to the structure and clarity these drafts offer. This increases productivity without sacrificing quality. By combining several jobs into a single process, workflow automation solutions go one step further. Users can rely on AI to follow present workflows rather than carrying out stages by hand.

An AI system might, for instance, accept data, clean it, analyses it, produce a report, and create a summary for approval. Every stage has a defined structure, which minimizes mistakes and delays. These kinds of technologies are particularly helpful for small groups and resource-constrained enterprises. Teams are able to manage higher workloads without adding more employees by automating routine procedures. Because tasks are carried out consistently, workflow automation also increases consistency. This is especially crucial in fields where consistency is crucial, such reporting, compliance, and documentation.

Scalability enhances these technologies' usefulness even more. As requirements increase, a system that functions well for a single class or small dataset may likewise manage heavier workloads. Because of this flexibility, businesses may begin small and grow over time, lowering risk and boosting confidence in the use of AI. All things considered; contemporary AI systems utilized in regular tasks have similar traits. They are approachable, easy to use, flexible, and problem-solving oriented. These technologies facilitate analysis, content production, and workflow automation, which improve productivity for both individuals and businesses. Their ability to blend in with daily tasks and produce reliable, significant results is what makes them valuable, not their technical prowess.

1.5 AI THAT ANSWERS VS. AI THAT DOES THE WORK

Nowadays, artificial intelligence is used in many different businesses, but depending on how it is used, its effects vary widely. Many firms think they are "using AI," yet the benefits they reap are minimal. This occurs because different applications of AI produce varying degrees of value. There is an important difference between AI that actively performs tasks and AI that delivers information. Anyone who wants to go beyond superficial adoption and realize genuine productivity increases must comprehend this distinction.

While question-answering AI is useful for learning and decision support, it frequently falls short of revolutionizing the way work is done. On the other hand, output, efficiency, and scalability are directly impacted by AI that does the task. The distinction between these two strategies determines whether AI develops into a true operational partner or stays a useful aid.

AI That Answers Questions

The most prevalent and well-known use of AI is question-answering AI. It gives definitions, summaries, explanations, or recommendations in response to requests. This kind of AI is particularly helpful when users require direction, clarity, or rapid comprehension of a subject. By cutting down on the amount of time needed to find information, it facilitates the processes of planning, thinking, and learning. For instance, a business analyst might question AI about typical consumer grievances within a specific sector. The AI has discovered patterns that allow it to characterize common problems. In a similar vein, a developer might ask AI to explain a programming topic, or a teacher might ask AI to create an efficient lesson plan. AI serves as a sophisticated reference tool in each of these situations. Despite its value, this type of AI is constrained by one important aspect: execution is still done by hand. The user still has to gather information, conduct analysis, create documents, and finish activities independently after obtaining it.

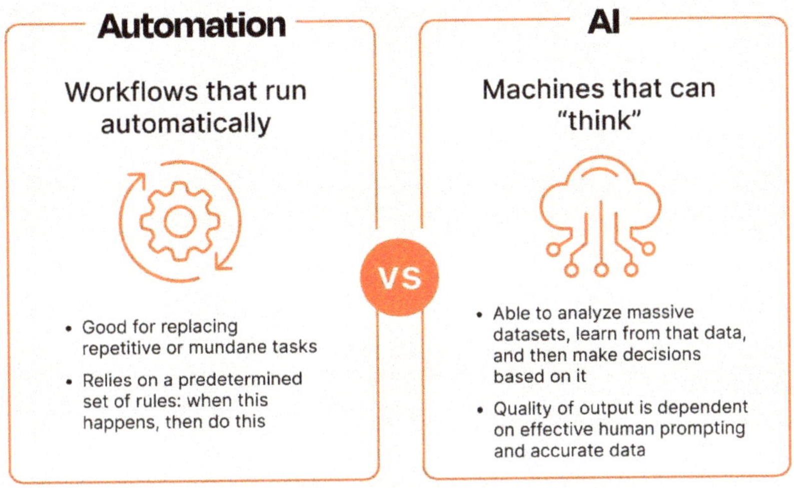

Figure 1.3: Difference between AI that provides answers and AI that performs complete tasks.

Source: *(Anna Burgess, 2025)*

Although AI facilitates comprehension, it does not lessen the effort required to produce finished goods. As a result, question-answering AI frequently advances knowledge without appreciably increasing productivity. It improves people's ability to think, but it has no significant effect on how much work they can perform in a given amount of time. Businesses that simply use this amount of AI may feel educated, but they may still feel overburdened by their everyday responsibilities.

AI That Does the Work

Work-doing AI functions at a deeper and more significant level. It follows systematic directions to perform activities from beginning to end or to a useable state, rather than merely providing information. Workflows incorporate this kind of AI, which actively processes inputs and produces outputs. For example, a team can upload survey data and provide AI instructions to clean responses, find themes, compile insights, and create a report draft rather than asking AI what stages are involved in survey analysis. In this case, AI is actually carrying out the process rather than merely discussing it.

The human role changes from performing monotonous tasks to evaluating and improving outcomes. The goal of work-based AI is results, not just explanations. It focuses on creating instantly usable texts, summaries, reports, analyses, or structured data. This method speeds up turnaround time and drastically lowers execution effort. Consistency is another crucial aspect of AI that does the task. Depending on who is doing the labor, how focused they are, and how much time they have, the results of manual activities can differ.

AI produces standardized results because it always follows the same instructions. This consistency is especially helpful when it comes to routine analysis, documentation, and reporting. Work-performing AI is also easily scalable. Once a workflow is established, it may be used for repeated operations or larger datasets without requiring correspondingly more work. Workloads that were previously exclusively manageable by larger organizations can now be handled by small teams.

Why the Difference Matters for Productivity

Productivity results are directly impacted by the difference between answering and doing. AI is still a helpful tool when it is solely employed to provide answers to queries. It becomes a productivity multiplier when it is put to work. Cutting down on execution time and effort is the key to true productivity gains.

A lot of organizational work is predictable, systematic, and repetitive. Although they demand a lot of human labor, these jobs don't always call for human ingenuity or discernment at every turn. AI is ideally equipped to manage such tasks effectively. Organizations free up human resources for higher-value work by letting AI handle execution-heavy tasks. Workers can concentrate on strategic thinking, decision-making, relationship-building, and interpretation.

As a result of spending less time on tedious chores, efficiency and job satisfaction both increase. The adoption of AI in organizations is also influenced by this divide. While work-based AI is incorporated into everyday operations, question-based AI is frequently utilized only infrequently. Stronger returns on investment and a deeper integration of AI into workflows follow over time.

Why This Book Focuses on AI That Does the Work

This book aims to take readers beyond the fundamentals of using AI. Although knowledge and comprehension are valuable, they don't change the way work is done on their own. When AI takes on the responsibility of completing certain steps in the workflow rather than merely providing advice, transformation takes place. Organizations can attain quantifiable results by concentrating on AI that does the work. Execution-focused AI offers measurable advantages such as reduced workload, scalability, consistency, and time savings. These advantages are particularly important for small IT teams, educational institutions, and survey-based businesses where efficiency is crucial and resources are scarce.

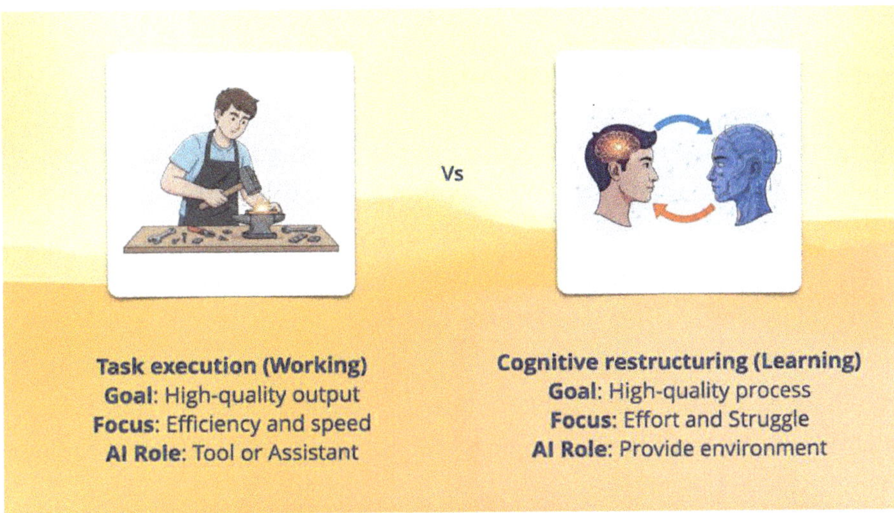

Figure 1.4: This Book Focuses on AI That Does the Work

The necessity for humans is not eliminated by this method. It reinterprets their role instead. Humans are still in charge of establishing objectives, formulating guidelines, evaluating results, and reaching judgments. The execution layer is handled by AI, which works under human-defined parameters. A fundamental first step in the practical use of AI is to comprehend the distinction between AI that answers and AI that performs the work. Expectations are changed from novelty to value and from access to information to actual operational impact.

1.6 PRACTICAL AI FOR SURVEY-BASED BUSINESSES

To make well-informed decisions, survey-based firms rely on input gathered from users, consumers, or staff. This input frequently comes in a variety of formats and in great quantities, particularly when surveys have open-ended questions. Even though this kind of data is very useful, it has historically been a difficult and time-consuming process to transform it into insightful knowledge. Survey data must be carefully cleaned, reviewed, categorized, and interpreted before being handled manually. These steps take time and increase the possibility of human mistake. These difficulties become increasingly more apparent as survey quantities increase. A potent support system for survey-driven companies is practical AI. By automating repetitious and data-intensive processes, it enhances human analysts' work rather than replaces it. Instead of spending days on mechanical processing, AI enables teams to concentrate on insight validation, interpretation, and client communication. The capacity of practical AI to improve survey operations' speed, consistency, and scalability is what really makes it valuable.

The Challenge of Manual Survey Processing

Seldom does survey data arrive in a clear, usable format. Spelling errors, incomplete responses, duplicate entries, and irrelevant content are all possible in responses. Each of these problems needs to be addressed when done by hand. Line by line, analysts must go through spread sheets, select which responses to include or leave out, and use their own discretion when classifying comparable comments. Because different team members may perceive results differently, this procedure is not only time-consuming but also inconsistent. Scale is another significant obstacle. It may still be possible to manually handle a small survey with a few hundred responses, but contemporary businesses sometimes handle thousands or even tens of thousands of responses. Fatigue increases with volume.

Mental fatigue over time may cause feedback to be misclassified or to miss trends. This has a direct impact on the caliber of insights provided to clients and erodes trust in the finished reports. Business growth is also constrained by manual processing. Scaling operations necessitates recruiting additional employees, raising expenses, and lengthening delivery timeframes when the amount of human labor required for each new project is comparable. This strategy is ineffective and unsustainable for survey-based companies that compete in markets.

How Practical AI Transforms Survey Workflows

By automating the most taxing steps of the workflow, practical AI transforms the way survey data is handled. Data cleansing is one of its main contributions. Artificial intelligence (AI) systems can swiftly search datasets for duplicates, missing values, and replies that don't match predetermined standards for quality. By ensuring that only trustworthy data is sent for analysis, this automated cleaning lowers the possibility of inaccurate results. AI is quite good at classifying replies and finding themes once the data is ready. Similar concepts presented in various ways are frequently seen in survey responses. AI can examine language trends throughout the entire dataset and group related responses together, eliminating the need for a human analyst to thoroughly read and interpret each response. A clear picture of what respondents are saying most frequently and what matters most is given by this thematic grouping.

AI facilitates insight summarization as well. AI can produce structured summaries that emphasize prominent trends, recurrent issues, and noteworthy variations, eliminating the need for analysts to manually distil hundreds of comments into essential points. These summaries facilitate teams' rapid transition from unprocessed data to insightful conclusions and provide a solid basis for more in-depth study. Report preparation is arguably one of the most significant applications of practical AI. Businesses that rely on surveys frequently have to produce polished, client-ready results on short notice. AI is capable of creating report parts, arranging data logically, and presenting findings in an expert manner. After that, human reviewers polish the wording, confirm interpretations, and make sure it complies with customer requirements. This cooperative method preserves quality while drastically cutting turnaround time.

Business Benefits and Long-Term Impact

Businesses that use surveys profit immediately and quantifiably from the use of practical AI. One of the most obvious enhancements is speed. Previously time-consuming tasks can frequently be finished in a matter of hours. In addition to improving customer happiness, faster delivery enables businesses to take on more projects without hiring more employees. Consistency is also another significant benefit. AI eliminates variance brought on by human judgment by applying the same guidelines and standards to all datasets. As a result, reports become more consistent and insights gain credibility. Over time, clients develop trust because they receive outputs with a consistent structure and quality level. Additionally, practical AI lessens internal tiredness and workload. Repetitive cleaning and sorting operations no longer require analysts to put in long hours. Alternatively, they can concentrate on client engagement, strategic advice, and interpretation.

As team members devote more time to intellectually stimulating work, this change not only boosts output but also job happiness. Scalability is made possible by AI from a growth standpoint. Larger projects and bigger response volumes can be undertaken by survey-based companies without correspondingly raising operating expenses. In a data-driven context, this scalability facilitates service expansion, market entry, and competitiveness. Above all, realistic AI does not eliminate the need for human skill. For final decision-making, ethical considerations, and contextual awareness, human judgment is still crucial. Humans can work more efficiently since AI just does the heavy lifting. Practical AI may be a reliable partner that improves survey operations and raises the total value provided to clients when used carefully. Businesses may overcome the constraints of manual processes and transition to a more effective, reliable, and sustainable model of insight generation by incorporating useful AI into survey operations.

1.7 PRACTICAL AI FOR EDUCATIONAL INSTITUTIONS

The demands and duties placed on educational institutions worldwide are steadily rising. Classroom instruction is no longer the only duty of teachers. They must plan interesting classes, create tests, analyses student achievement, keep track of documents, interact with parents, and assist students with a range of learning requirements. In contrast, administrators are responsible for overseeing academic planning, compliance, reporting, and communication while maintaining efficient day-to-day operations. A large portion of this labor takes place after school hours, which raises stress levels and limits the amount of time teachers can spend interacting meaningfully with kids.

To tackle these issues, practical artificial intelligence provides a workable solution. Practical AI places more emphasis on tools that directly support everyday administrative and academic duties than it does on sophisticated technology or experimental systems. These resources are made to be simple to use, necessitate little technological expertise, and blend in seamlessly with current teaching methods. When applied carefully, practical AI turns into a tool that boosts productivity without undermining education's emphasis on people.

AI Support for Teaching and Academic Activities

Lesson preparation is one of the most time-consuming tasks for educators. It takes careful planning to create lesson plans that match curricular requirements, learning objectives, and student capacities. By creating structured lesson plans according to grade levels and subject needs, practical AI can help. These outlines can then be modified by teachers in accordance with their pedagogical approach and classroom setting. This preserves the quality of training while cutting down on preparation time. Another area where practical AI is useful is in assignment generation. Instructors frequently have to create practice questions, homework assignments, and worksheets that support learning objectives. Draft assignments that are suited to particular subjects or skill levels can be produced by AI systems.

Teachers who are teaching several classes or subjects will find this very useful. Instead of starting from scratch, instructors can concentrate on personalizing the curriculum by starting with AI-generated drafts. Grading and assessment can require a lot of work, especially in big class sizes. By going over student responses, pointing out frequent mistakes, and recommending initial assessments based on present standards, practical AI can help. AI cuts down on the amount of time spent on tedious evaluation chores, but teachers still have the final say in grading.

This enables teachers to give more insightful comments rather than just concentrating on grades. Monitoring performance is yet another crucial scholarly endeavor. Teachers are frequently expected to track students' development over time and spot learning gaps early. To find trends in student performance, AI algorithms can examine participation data and evaluation results. These insights assist teachers in determining which pupils can benefit from extra guidance and which subjects need to be revised. Teachers can more successfully modify their instruction using this knowledge.

Administrative Efficiency and Communication Enhancement

Educational institutions require a lot of administrative work in addition to teaching. Reporting, recordkeeping, and communication take up a lot of time for educators and administrators. Despite being necessary, these assignments frequently interfere with academic engagement. By automating repetitive administrative tasks, practical AI helps to streamline these procedures. One of the main administrative duties in schools and universities is reporting. Accurate and consistent information is necessary for compliance documentation, internal evaluations, and academic progress reports. AI tools can help with data organization, key point summarization, and the creation of structured draft reports. Although the burden required to prepare these materials is greatly decreased, human inspection guarantees correctness and appropriateness.

Another crucial component of education is parent-teacher communication. Parents anticipate receiving timely information regarding school events, attendance, and academic success. It can be very taxing to draft separate messages or reports for every kid. Teachers can customize clear and consistent communication templates created by practical AI before sending them. This minimizes tedious writing processes while guaranteeing openness. AI helps administrators with internal communication, scheduling, and collaboration as well. AI can help with notice or announcement preparation, meeting discussion summarization, and academic calendar organization. These technologies lessen the possibility that crucial details will be missed and help to ensure consistency in communication. Standardization is a significant benefit of using AI in administration. Output quality increases when tasks like communication and reporting adhere to standard formats.

Students, parents, and staff are less confused as a result of this consistency, which also increases the institution's trustworthiness. AI in practice does not replace human intervention. Empathy, discernment, and moral decision-making are critical in educational settings. AI facilitates these settings by managing repetitive and regimented duties, freeing up administrators and teachers to concentrate on people rather than paperwork. The way that practical AI transforms time usage is where its real value in educational institutions rests. AI frees up educators to concentrate on teaching, mentoring, and student development by easing administrative workloads and assisting with academic preparation. While adjusting to the needs of the current world, this harmony between technology and human knowledge guarantees that education is effective, inclusive, and personalized.

1.8 PRACTICAL AI FOR SMALL TECH TEAMS

The climate in which small technical teams work is one of constant pressure. They must work with a small team, strict deadlines, and limited resources to design, develop, test, deploy, and manage software products. Small tech teams cannot afford distinct roles for requirements analysis, documentation, testing, and release management, in contrast to large enterprises. Because of this, engineers and team leads frequently juggle a lot of tasks, which impairs focus and raises the possibility of mistakes and burnout.

Artificial intelligence in practice provides a workable answer to these problems. Practical AI serves as a helpful helper that assists teams in handling repetitive and ordinary activities rather than introducing sophisticated systems or taking the place of human expertise. Without adding more employees or complicating operations, small IT teams may increase productivity, maintain quality, and grow output by incorporating AI into regular workflows.

AI Support across the Development Lifecycle

Managing requirements and feature requests is one of the first difficulties small tech teams encounter. Frequently, input comes from a variety of sources, including emails, support tickets, customer reviews, and internal conversations. It requires time and careful consideration to transform this unstructured data into requirements that are both clear and actionable. By analyzing unstructured data and condensing them into requirement descriptions, practical AI can help. This minimizes misunderstandings during development and aids teams in rapidly understanding what needs to be built.

Boilerplate code, typical logic structures, and common error handling are examples of repeating patterns that developers commonly encounter during the coding phase. By providing other implementations, pointing out possible problems, and suggesting code snippets, Practical AI assists developers. This speeds up execution and lessens mental strain, but it does not take the place of the developer's involvement in architecture design or technical decision-making. Developers can spend less time on standard syntax and more time solving problems. Another area that frequently gets less attention in small teams because of time restrictions is documentation.

However, cooperation, on boarding, and maintenance all depend on accurate documentation. By examining feature descriptions, commit messages, or code comments, practical AI can assist in producing preliminary technical documentation drafts. Developers can examine and improve upon the solid foundation these drafts offer. Consequently, documentation remains current without adding to the workload. AI assistance is also advantageous for testing and quality control. Careful analysis is necessary for creating test cases, determining edge scenarios, and summarizing issue reports. Teams can increase test coverage by using practical AI to generate test case ideas based on requirements and code behavior.

It can also help with bug report organization by providing a clear and uniform summary of issues. This methodical approach expedites problem solving and lessens misunderstanding. Another ongoing duty in the development lifecycle is release communication. It takes time to prepare deployment messages, release notes, and update summaries, particularly when releases occur frequently. By evaluating finished tasks and modifications, Practical AI may produce draft release notes. Teams may swiftly share updates with stakeholders and users thanks to these drafts, which also guarantee consistency in communication.

Reducing Pressure and Enabling Sustainable Productivity

Beyond specific tasks, practical AI's true influence is seen in the way it changes small tech teams' daily work routines. Developers encounter fewer context shifts when AI supports repetitive tasks. They can stay focused for longer stretches of time rather than bouncing back and forth between coding, documentation, reporting, and communication. Both productivity and the caliber of the job are enhanced by this. Additionally, practical AI lessens reliance on individual team members. Knowledge is frequently concentrated among a limited number of individuals in small teams. Information becomes more consistent and accessible when AI helps with reporting, summarization, and documentation. This enhances teamwork generally and lowers risk when team members are missing.

AI assistance is also useful in sprint planning and work prioritization. It might be difficult for small teams to strike a balance between short-term fixes and long-term enhancements. Task lists may be streamlined, dependencies can be highlighted, and organized summaries of forthcoming work can be produced with the use of practical AI. This encourages more effective planning conversations and saves teams from having to spend too much time organizing information in order to make well-informed decisions. Scalability is a key benefit of adopting AI as a helper. Small teams are frequently under pressure to produce more with fewer resources when client demands or product usage rise. By automating support jobs instead of increasing staff size, practical AI helps companies manage increased workloads. This permits expansion without adding overhead in communication or management complexity.

It is crucial to remember that real AI does not eliminate the need for human judgment. Humans are still in charge of system architecture, security concerns, strategic choices, and moral obligations. AI does not provide ownership; it supports execution. This equilibrium fosters a fruitful collaboration between people and technology when applied appropriately. Additionally, practical AI supports long-term sustainability. In tech teams, persistent overwork causes burnout and high turnover. AI contributes to a healthy workplace by lowering administrative stress and repetitive workload. This increases employment satisfaction and retention by allowing developers to devote more time to learning, creativity, and relevant technical challenges.

Adoption must be gradual and deliberate for practical AI to be effective. When AI is implemented gradually, beginning with low-risk jobs like task summaries or documentation drafts, small tech teams stand to gain the most. AI can be incorporated into increasingly intricate procedures as trust increases. This strategy guarantees consistency and fosters confidence in AI-assisted procedures. Being efficient in small IT teams doesn't mean doing everything faster at all costs. It's about making prudent use of scarce resources. By producing dependable software and preserving equilibrium and clarity in day-to-day tasks, practical AI allows teams to concentrate their efforts where they are most needed.

1.9 GETTING STARTED WITH A PRACTICAL AI MIND-SET

Successfully implementing artificial intelligence is more of a mentality issue than a technological one. Assuming that automation will instantaneously address every issue, many firms have irrational expectations and rush toward AI. Teams frequently get confused, disappointed, and resistant as a result of this strategy. A realistic AI mentality understands that AI is a helpful tool that adds value when used carefully and progressively rather than a panacea.

Successful AI-enabled organizations start by changing their perspective on work. They ask where AI can actually save time, enhance consistency, and minimize effort rather than how much can be automated. This change in perspective helps teams feel confident rather than intimidated by new technology and lays a solid basis for long-term AI adoption.

Starting with Small, Meaningful Use Cases

Starting small is the first step toward adopting a realistic AI mentality. Making an initial attempt to automate intricate or crucial procedures frequently results in needless risk. The first step in practical adoption is to identify time-consuming, repetitive, uncomplicated jobs that don't demand complex judgment. Regardless of size or sector, these tasks are present in all organizations. Routine document drafting, information summarization, data organization, report preparation, and basic analysis assistance are a few examples. The advantages of using AI for these kinds of activities become apparent very soon. Repetitive tasks are instantly relieved for teams, which increases technology trust. Early success is essential for fostering favorable perceptions of AI.

Organizations can also observe how AI performs in real-world scenarios by starting small. Teams discover which inputs result in superior results and when human inspection is required. It is impossible to avoid this learning process. A practical attitude recognizes that improvement occurs via application rather than theory and prioritizes learning above perfection. Small use cases also have the benefit of less resistance. Employees are more willing to use AI when it is presented as a tool rather than a replacement. This transparency fosters creativity and turns the adoption of AI into a team effort rather than a directive.

Experimentation and Gradual Adoption

Experimentation is welcomed in a pragmatic AI perspective. AI tools get better with use, criticism, and improvement. Businesses that view AI as a fixed system frequently face difficulties, whereas those who view it as a dynamic helper see greater success. Teams can try various strategies, improve instructions, and modify procedures without feeling rushed by experimentation. Experimentation is strongly related to gradual adoption. Successful firms increase the use of AI gradually rather than implementing it across all departments at once. Similar tasks can be added when one task has been reliably automated. This planned growth guarantees quality maintenance and lowers risk.

Additionally, skill development is supported by gradual adoption. Over time, team members become increasingly proficient in interacting with AI. They enhance their ability to define tasks, evaluate results, and spot areas that could use improvement. These abilities are equally as crucial as the actual tools. Crucially, slow adoption maintains AI in line with corporate objectives. Leaders can track the effects, get input, and change course when changes are implemented gradually. This strategy guarantees AI stays applicable to actual job needs and keeps it from turning into a disjointed experiment.

Balancing Human Judgment and AI Execution

Understanding the role of humans is one of the most important components of a realistic AI mindset. Although AI is very good at structured, repetitive, and data-intensive activities, it is devoid of ethical reasoning, empathy, and context. In terms of responsibility, interpretation, and decision-making, human judgment is still crucial. Companies should specify exactly what AI is meant to do and when human supervision is needed. AI may create drafts, evaluate information, and offer insights; but, results need to be reviewed, improved, and approved by humans. This equilibrium fosters trust and keeps automation from becoming overly dependent.

Keeping human control also helps employees feel less afraid. Adoption goes more smoothly when people realize that AI is meant to supplement human labor, not to replace it. Openness on AI's function promotes safe use and helps to foster confidence. A pragmatic approach understands that human-AI cooperation yields the best outcomes. While people concentrate on strategy, creativity, and connections, AI manages execution support. Productivity is increased by this collaboration without sacrificing ideals or quality.

Continuous Improvement as a Long-Term Approach

Adoption of AI is a continual process as opposed to a one-time event. A pragmatic view of AI puts continuous improvement ahead of immediate benefits. As workflows evolve, AI policies, templates, and practices must be enhanced. Regular evaluation ensures AI's sustained efficacy as data, requirements, and goals change. Organizations should encourage users who frequently interact with AI to contribute. Their experience reveals what works and what needs to be changed. Over time, small, frequent adjustments greatly improve efficiency and reliability. Another component of continuous development is reevaluating assumptions. As confidence and understanding grow tasks that were once unsuited for automation may later become possible. Businesses that adopt a flexible strategy can gradually and ethically expand their usage of AI. Organizations generate lasting value when they see AI as a long-term collaborator rather than a temporary fix.

This kind of thinking guarantees that the use of AI improves processes, helps people, and changes with the times rather than becoming disruptive or outdated. In the end, a pragmatic AI mentality changes how businesses approach their work. It substitutes curiosity for fear, patience for pressure, and confidence for exploration. When AI is implemented carefully, it becomes a reliable ally in daily tasks, subtly increasing productivity while maintaining strong control over human judgment.

A. SHORT QUESTIONS

1. What is meant by practical AI?
2. Why AI was previously considered unrealistic for small organizations?
3. How has cloud-based technology changed AI adoption?
4. What is the difference between practical AI and theoretical AI?
5. Mention two everyday problems that AI can solve in organizations.
6. How does practical AI help survey-driven businesses?
7. In what ways can AI support educational institutions?
8. How does AI assist small tech teams in daily operations?
9. What is meant by AI that "does the work"?
10. Why is a practical AI mind-set important for organizations?

B. LONG QUESTIONS

1. Explain the concept of practical AI and discuss why it is more relevant today than in the past.
2. Describe how AI has moved beyond large enterprises and become accessible to small teams and organizations.
3. Discuss the role of practical AI in survey-based businesses with suitable examples.
4. Explain the difference between AI that answers questions and AI that performs complete tasks.
5. Describe how adopting a practical AI mind-set can improve productivity and efficiency in organizations.

C. MULTIPLE CHOICE QUESTIONS (MCQS)

1. Practical AI mainly focuses on:

   a) Theoretical research **b)** Answering complex questions
   c) Completing real work tasks **d)** Developing algorithms

2. Earlier AI adoption was difficult mainly because of:

   a) Lack of internet **b)** Expensive infrastructure and skilled talent
   c) Lack of software tools **d)** User resistance

3. Which of the following is a key feature of modern AI tools?

   a) Offline-only usage **b)** Designed only for programmers
   c) Cloud-based accessibility **d)** Hardware dependency

4. AI that answers questions is mainly useful for:

   a) Execution of workflows **b)** Providing information
   c) Automating tasks **d)** Eliminating human effort

5. Which example best represents AI that does the work?

   a) Explaining survey analysis steps **b)** Defining customer satisfaction
   c) Generating a complete survey report **d)** Answering customer queries

6. Practical AI helps small teams mainly by:

   a) Replacing employees **b)** Increasing workload
   c) Reducing manual effort **d)** Adding complexity

7. In educational institutions, practical AI is commonly used for:

   a) Hiring teachers **b)** Lesson planning and grading support
   c) Building infrastructure **d)** Student discipline

8. One major benefit of practical AI is:

   a) Increased confusion **b)** Reduced consistency
   c) Time and effort savings **d)** Higher costs

9. AI that performs tasks usually works through:

a) Random responses
b) Structured workflows
c) Manual instructions only
d) Trial and error

10. A practical AI mind-set encourages organizations to:

a) Automate everything immediately
b) Avoid human involvement
c) Start small and scale gradually
d) Use AI only for experiments

CHAPTER 2

AUTOMATING SURVEY-DRIVEN BUSINESSES

2.1 UNDERSTANDING SURVEY-DRIVEN BUSINESS MODELS

The core function of survey-driven firms is gathering feedback and turning it into insightful knowledge. These businesses leverage information obtained from clients, staff, users, or certain target audiences. Customer satisfaction surveys, employee involvement forms, market research questionnaires, product reviews, and service assessments can all provide feedback. The objective is always the same, regardless of the source: to comprehend viewpoints, experiences, and expectations and then effectively convey those conclusions to clients or decision-makers. The operational cycle of the majority of survey-driven enterprises is similar.

Initially, they use digital technologies to create and distribute surveys. After that, they gather answers over a predetermined time frame. The real job starts when the data is collected. Teams must examine the replies, spot patterns, and create dashboards or reports that provide a concise and useful summary of the results. Clients are then given access to these results in order to assist with choices, enhancements, or strategic planning. Although this methodology seems simple, the difficulty is in successfully managing and understanding the data, not in gathering it.

The Challenge of Data Overload

Managing responses by hand may seem doable in the early phases of survey-based work. However, data volume rises quickly as projects or enterprises expand. Larger research can yield thousands of responses, but even a simple poll can yield hundreds. Open-ended remarks that call for close reading and analysis may be included in each response. Data overload is a syndrome brought on by this surplus of data. Teams become less productive when they are presented with too much information at once. Large amounts of literature must be read, pertinent parts must be found, and related responses must be mentally grouped together.

In addition to taking a long time, this technique is mentally taxing. Fatigue reduces attention to detail, which raises the risk of mistakes or overlooked discoveries. Turnaround time is also impacted by data overload. Customers frequently anticipate speedy outcomes, yet manual analysis causes delivery delays. Teams may speed through reviews as a result, further jeopardizing quality and accuracy.

Inconsistency in Human Interpretation

Inconsistent interpretation is another significant issue with survey-driven business strategies. Divergent viewpoints inevitably emerge when several team members collaborate on the same dataset. A reaction can be seen as a minor problem by one analyst and a major concern by another. Different people may interpret context, tone, and linguistic subtleties differently. Reports of varying quality are the result of this inconsistency. Clients may observe differences between projects in terms of emphasis, organization, or depth of knowledge. This may eventually have an impact on credibility and trust. Survey-driven enterprises, particularly those that provide regular reports or long-term studies, need to be consistent. Maintaining consistency with manual analysis is challenging, especially when deadlines are tight or workloads are heavy.

The Role of AI in Survey-Driven Models

Artificial intelligence's capacity to efficiently and reliably handle massive amounts of text makes it an ideal fit for survey-driven business models. AI does not get tired or lose focus like humans do. It ensures consistent data handling by analyzing thousands of responses using the same criteria each time. AI is quite good at finding patterns in unstructured text. It can identify reoccurring themes, cluster related answers, and draw attention to problems that are brought up regularly. By lowering the quantity of unprocessed data that people must examine, this feature directly tackles the issue of data overload. Analysts can concentrate on examining condensed insights and verifying results rather of reading each individual response. As a result, human labor is redirected from manual processing to quality control and interpretation, where human judgment is most useful.

Improving Efficiency and Scalability

Because additional data volume necessitates more human labor, survey-driven firms frequently find it difficult to grow. In addition to raising expenses, hiring more analysts may not necessarily ensure constant quality. This relationship is altered by AI, which allows companies to manage more data without correspondingly growing their workforces. The same team can handle more clients, more projects, and quicker turnaround times with AI support. Delivery schedules get better and workflows become more predictable. For small and medium-sized survey companies looking to expand without going over budget, this scalability is especially crucial. Teams may spend more time honing insights, enhancing report quality, and interacting with clients thanks to efficiency advantages. Teams can concentrate on providing value instead of being overtaken by data.

Why AI Complements Human Expertise

AI cannot take the position of human analysts in survey-driven organizations. Making strategic advice, deciphering complex meanings, and comprehending context all require human knowledge. AI eliminates the burden of time-consuming, repetitive tasks that reduce human productivity. AI frees up analysts to use their expertise where it matters most by managing text processing and pattern recognition. When AI and humans work together, the results are superior to when they operate alone.

This equilibrium is very beneficial to survey-driven business models. While humans guarantee the quality and applicability of insights, AI guarantees consistency and speed. When combined, they create a feedback analysis method that is more robust and scalable. Organizations that wish to stay competitive in a data-driven environment must comprehend this connection between AI capabilities and survey-driven procedures.

2.2 COMMON CHALLENGES IN MANUAL SURVEY PROCESSING

For many organizations, especially survey-driven companies that frequently deal with high volumes of input, manual survey processing remains a significant operational burden. Even while digital tools have made it easier than ever to gather replies, a significant amount of human labor is still required to transform survey data into insightful and trustworthy conclusions. Project schedules, team productivity, and customer satisfaction are all directly impacted by this dependency's delays, inconsistencies, and quality problems. The manual workload rises quickly when surveys have hundreds or thousands of responses. Data must be cleaned, each response must be examined, patterns must be found, and reports must be refined. Time, focus, and consistency are required for each of these tasks. The limits of manual processing become more apparent as workloads increase.

Data Preparation and Quality Challenges

The first major difficulty in manual survey processing appears during data preparation. Survey datasets are rarely clean when they arrive. They often include duplicated entries, incomplete responses, spelling errors, and irrelevant or off-topic answers. Preparing such data for analysis requires careful review of each response to ensure that only valid and useful information is retained.

1. **Time-Consuming Data Cleaning**: Cleaning survey data manually requires analysts to scan row by row, check response completeness, and remove duplicates. As response volume grows, this process becomes increasingly slow. What should

be a short preparatory step can extend into several hours or even days, delaying the entire analysis workflow.

2. **High Risk of Human Error**: Manual data cleaning is prone to mistakes caused by fatigue and oversight. Valid responses may be removed accidentally, while irrelevant data may remain unnoticed. Since survey insights rely heavily on data quality, even small errors at this stage can distort findings and reduce the reliability of results.
3. **Inconsistent Judgment across Team Members**: Different team members may apply slightly different criteria while cleaning data. One analyst may consider a response usable, while another may discard it. This inconsistency affects data quality and makes it difficult to maintain uniform standards across projects.

Analysis, Interpretation, and Reporting Limitations

Once the data is cleaned, the next challenge lies in analysis and reporting. Open-ended survey responses provide valuable qualitative insights, but they are also the hardest to process manually. Each response may express similar ideas using different language, tone, or context.

1. **Difficulty in Identifying Themes**: Manually identifying recurring themes requires careful reading and interpretation of every response. Analysts must compare responses continuously to detect patterns such as pricing concerns, usability issues, or service dissatisfaction. As the number of responses increases, maintaining accuracy and consistency becomes difficult.
2. **Lack of Scalability**: Manual analysis does not scale well. A team that can comfortably analyze a few hundred responses may struggle significantly when dealing with thousands. The workload increases linearly with data size, while human capacity does not. This often forces businesses to delay delivery or reduce the depth of analysis.
3. **Mental Fatigue and Reduced Consistency**: Reading large volumes of text repeatedly leads to cognitive fatigue. Over time, analysts may miss subtle patterns or interpret similar responses differently. This reduces consistency in theme categorization and weakens the reliability of insights.
4. **Complex and Time-Intensive Report Preparation**: Transforming insights into client-ready reports requires structuring content, summarizing findings, and presenting results clearly. Multiple revisions are often needed to refine language, incorporate feedback, and adjust formatting. This stage alone can take as much time as the analysis itself.

5. **Inconsistent Presentation Quality**: When reports are prepared manually by different team members, variations in writing style, structure, and level of detail are common. This inconsistency affects brand perception and reduces client confidence, especially when comparing reports across projects or time periods.
6. **Operational Strain on Teams**: The combined effect of manual cleaning, analysis, and reporting places heavy strain on teams. Employees spend most of their time on repetitive tasks, leaving little room for deeper analysis, strategic thinking, or client engagement. Over time, fatigue increases and overall productivity declines.

Artificial intelligence addresses these challenges by automating the most repetitive and time-consuming steps of survey processing. By supporting data preparation, pattern recognition, and draft generation, AI reduces delays and minimizes errors while allowing human experts to remain in control of final decisions.

2.3 CLEANING AND PREPARING SURVEY DATA USING AI

Data preparation is the foundation of the entire analysis process in survey-driven enterprises. Unreliable data always produces poor results, regardless of how sophisticated reporting or insight-generation technologies are. Large numbers of survey responses are typically received, and they frequently include irrelevant content, spelling errors, duplicate entries, missing answers, and formatting problems. It takes a lot of time and mental energy to solve these issues by hand, and even seasoned teams find it difficult to stay consistent across projects. This level is transformed by practical AI, which brings uniform standards, speed, and accuracy. AI enhances human judgment by effectively managing repetitious preparation chores rather than replacing it. Teams may be confident that only significant and trustworthy answers advance to analysis, reporting, and decision-making when data cleaning is automated.

How AI Handles Raw Survey Data

Spreadsheet formats like CSV or Excel files are commonly used to collect survey data. The system first concentrates on comprehending the dataset's structure when these files are added to an AI-assisted workflow. Without the need for human configuration, AI rapidly analyzes column headings, recognizes answer kinds, and finds patterns. The system can process data intelligently instead of mechanically thanks to this basic understanding. AI verifies the data against expected formats and logical rules after identifying the structure. AI examines the entire dataset at once, detecting items that don't fulfill fundamental quality standards, as opposed to manually scanning rows one at a time. This method saves time and lowers the possibility of missing important problems due to oversight or exhaustion.AI is also essential for spotting redundant answers. Technical issues, repetitive imports, or multiple submissions can all result in duplicate entries. These duplicates have the potential to skew results and mislead real feedback if they persist. To precisely identify duplicates, AI checks timestamps, IDs, and response patterns. It can either automatically eliminate these entries or flag them for human review based on predetermined standards, guaranteeing that each response is tallied only once.

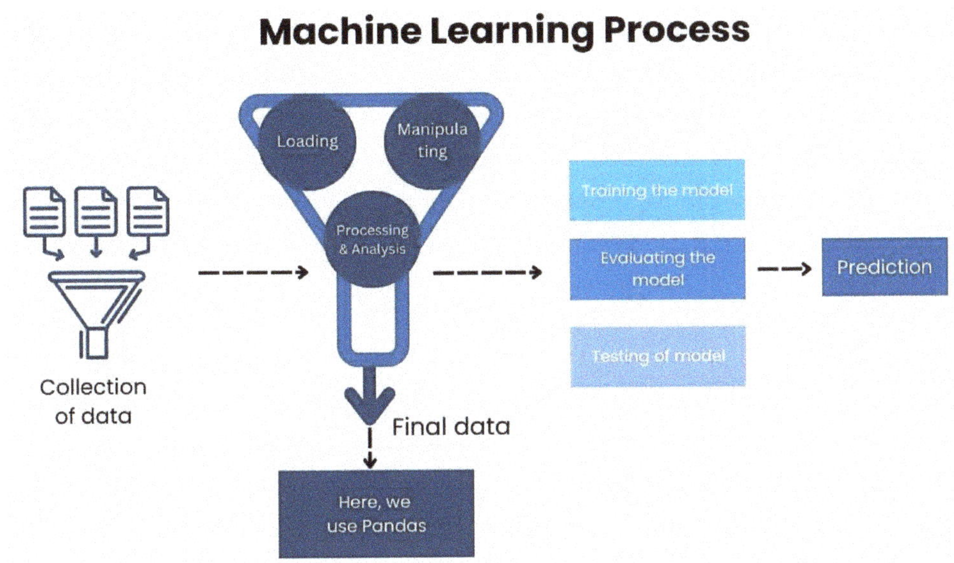

Figure 2.1: Automated cleaning and validation of raw survey data using AI tools.

Another area where AI adds consistency is in the handling of partial and incorrect responses. Some survey respondents supply insufficient information, submit irrelevant content, or leave questions unfilled. Various team members may use various inclusion or exclusion criteria when working manually. AI ensures fairness and dependability in data preparation by applying same rules to all datasets.

AI-driven validation ensures data quality by:

- Flagging responses that miss mandatory fields critical for analysis
- Detecting entries that do not match expected formats or logical patterns
- Separating usable responses from low-quality or unreliable submissions

This structured filtering allows analysts to work with confidence, knowing the dataset meets predefined standards.

Reducing Noise and Creating Reliable Data for Analysis

Noise is frequently introduced into datasets via open-ended survey questions. Respondents might write jokes, irrelevant remarks, or off-topic remarks. Although such responses can be recognized by humans, it is ineffective to do so across thousands of submissions. AI looks for text that deviates from the purpose of the query by analyzing linguistic patterns and contextual relevance. It is possible to reduce clutter and enhance analytical clarity by filtering out or classifying these responses independently. Inconsistency in wording is another significant problem with survey data. The same problem may be described by different individuals using different wording, phrasing, or spelling. AI normalizes text and fixes glaring mistakes to standardize responses. Later phases like theme identification and insight extraction are made easier by this standardization, which guarantees that related concepts are appropriately put together rather than handled as distinct problems .A smaller but much more dependable dataset is the result of AI-based cleaning and preparation.

Before analysis starts, hidden mistakes, duplication, and deceptive entries are eliminated. This greatly increases the precision of insights and boosts trust in the results that are given to stakeholders or clients. Automated cleaning also lessens mental stress for people. The repetitious and taxing nature of manual data preparation frequently results in a gradual loss of attention. AI regularly completes these jobs without getting tired, freeing up team members to concentrate on communication, interpretation, and strategic thinking. This change increases job satisfaction in addition to productivity. Above all, clean data establishes a solid basis for automation. Analysis, reporting, and visualization powered by AI are totally dependent on structured inputs. The entire process becomes quicker, more scalable, and more reliable when AI effectively handles data preparation. Then, survey-based companies can manage bigger datasets, fulfill deadlines, and consistently provide high-quality insights without sacrificing accuracy or credibility.

2.4 IDENTIFYING THEMES AND PATTERNS AUTOMATICALLY

Open-ended questions are frequently used by survey-driven enterprises to gather sincere thoughts, feelings, and experiences. Although these answers offer deep qualitative insights, they also pose a significant problem. It becomes challenging to determine what really important when hundreds or thousands of people express their ideas in their own terms. Analysts used to have to carefully study each response, underline important details, and manually group related concepts. This is a laborious, tedious process that heavily relies on personal interpretation. This is entirely changed when AI is used to automatically identify themes and patterns. AI can quickly and reliably assess vast amounts of open-ended survey replies once the data has been prepped and cleaned. It is not fatigued, sidetracked, or affected by expectations. Instead, it focuses purely on the language and meaning within the data, making thematic analysis far more efficient and reliable.

How AI Identifies Themes in Open-Ended Responses

AI differs from humans in how it handles open-ended survey responses. It examines each response's structure, language, and context rather than reading it word by word. Even when people use various words or idioms to explain problems, it finds commonalities in their descriptions. For instance, "high cost" may be mentioned by one respondent, "too expensive" by another, and "pricing issues" by a third. All of these answers lead to the same underlying concept, according to AI. AI automatically creates meaningful clusters from comparable input by processing the full dataset at once. Themes including pricing issues, customer service encounters, product usability, delivery speed, or general contentment are frequently represented by these clusters. Regardless of the amount of the dataset, this categorization occurs consistently across projects.

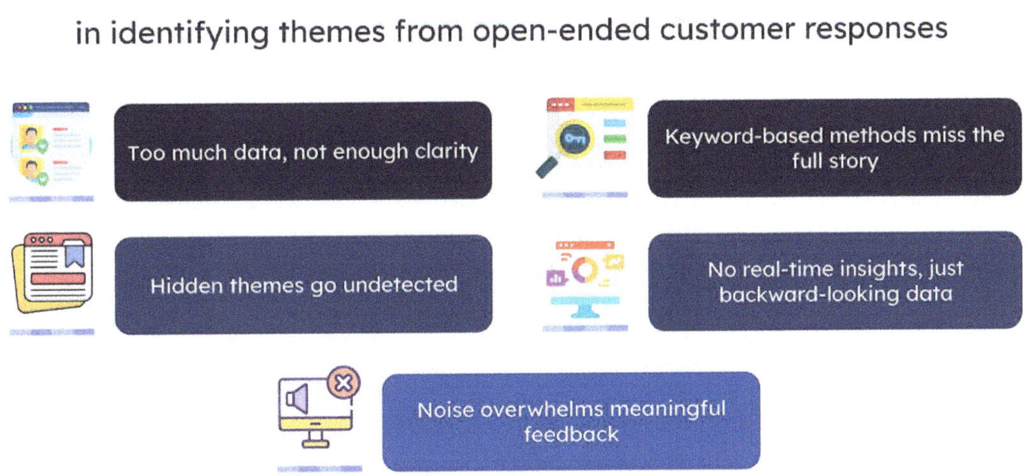

Figure 2.2: Identification of themes and patterns in open-ended survey responses using AI.

The outcomes are consistent and similar over time because AI applies the same reasoning to each response. Human bias, a significant drawback of manual analysis, is also eliminated by this computerized procedure. When analyzing input, people could unintentionally concentrate on problems they anticipate or ignore trends that contradict their presumptions. Such expectations do not apply to AI. It produces more objective results by identifying themes only on the basis of frequency, linguistic patterns, and contextual similarities.

Ensuring Consistency and Scalability across Projects

Consistency is one of the main benefits of AI-driven theme detection. Different analysts may classify the same response differently in a manual analysis. Feedback can be interpreted differently by the same person on various days. It is challenging to compare survey data or monitor trends over time due to this unpredictability. By using the same analytical method each time, AI solves this issue. AI uses the same standards to assess survey responses, regardless of the number of responses 10,000 or 100,000. This guarantees that themes found in one project can be directly compared to those found in another. This consistency is also important for survey-driven companies that manage recurrent client work. Another important advantage is scalability. The amount of survey data rises as companies expand. Because manual thematic analysis involves more personnel and time, it does not scale effectively. Larger datasets, however, may be processed by AI with little more work. This enables companies to take on additional tasks without adding to their workload or sacrificing quality.

Shifting the Analyst's Role from Reading to Validation

The function of human analysts is positively altered when theme identification is handled by AI. Analysts can concentrate on examining condensed themes and confirming their applicability rather than devoting hours to analyzing individual comments. Efficiency and insight quality are both enhanced by this change. The themes produced by AI are examined by analysts to make sure they make sense in the context. If necessary, they can combine closely related themes, modify labels, or divide large categories into more focused ones. By combining human judgment with AI's processing capability, this cooperative method produces more precise and significant discoveries.

AI frees analysts from tedious reading so they can devote more time to interpretation and narrative. They can investigate the reasons for the emergence of particular themes, their connection to corporate choices, and suggested courses of action. This improves the value provided to clients and raises the general standard of survey analysis. Thus, automatic theme and pattern recognition is both a technical and strategic advancement. While maintaining the crucial role of human expertise, it revolutionizes how survey-driven firms manage qualitative data by making analysis quicker, more reliable, and more insightful.

2.5 EXTRACTING INSIGHTS FROM LARGE RESPONSE SETS

Gathering survey data is just the beginning of learning what customers think. The insights that can be gained from feedback are what make it truly valuable. It gets harder for businesses to manually find significant patterns when they receive hundreds or thousands of responses. Significant signals are easily overlooked, and analysis frequently becomes inconsistent amongst analysts. Practical AI is crucial in this situation because it converts unprocessed replies into understandable, useful insights that facilitate improved decision-making. AI is more than just theme recognition. Large answer sets are analyzed holistically, exposing patterns, emotional tone, and reoccurring problems that could otherwise go unnoticed. By doing this, AI helps companies go beyond just knowing what customers have to say to comprehend the true significance of those responses.

Understanding Trends and Patterns in Feedback

Subtle trends that are not apparent when examining individual responses are sometimes found in large datasets. AI examines every response collectively and finds recurrent themes, changes in viewpoint, and new issues over time. This enables companies to observe trends that emerge over several weeks, months, or consumer groups. AI might identify, for instance, that while customer satisfaction with product quality has been continuously high, concerns over delivery delays have significantly increased over recent polls.

These insights assist businesses in comprehending not just the current situation but also the evolving perceptions of their customers. Because trend analysis distinguishes between regions that are stable and those that need immediate attention, it becomes particularly useful for long-term planning. By identifying these patterns automatically, AI removes the burden of manual comparison and reduces the risk of overlooking critical developments.

Sentiment and Frequency Analysis for Deeper Insight

Beyond identifying topics, AI can evaluate the emotional tone of responses. Sentiment analysis helps distinguish between positive, negative, and neutral feedback, providing a clearer picture of customer satisfaction. This emotional component deepens the analysis and aids companies in comprehending how strongly consumers feel about particular problems. AI also calculates frequency, which shows how frequently particular subjects come up in responses. When sentiment and frequency are combined, the results become highly actionable. For instance, a topic that appears frequently with strong negative sentiment signals an urgent problem, while a less frequent but highly positive topic may represent a key strength. These insights allow organizations to prioritize actions effectively. Rather of responding to isolated remarks, teams can focus on issues that impact the largest number of customers and generate the strongest emotional responses.

Turning Insights into Business Value

Only when extracted insights direct action are they beneficial. AI-generated insights assist companies in converting customer comments into useful suggestions. Organizations can match their strategy with actual customer needs by precisely understanding what customers enjoy and dislike. For instance, businesses can prioritize enhancing support procedures without altering the product itself if AI indicates that the majority of negative feedback pertains to response time while positive feedback constantly highlights product quality. This focused strategy guarantees that resources are allocated where they are most needed and avoids needless modifications. Additionally, AI enhances the caliber of reports that are presented to clients.

Businesses can provide targeted insights that concisely illustrate important concerns and opportunities rather than offering raw data or long summaries. Because the analysis is clear, supported by data, and in line with their objectives, clients benefit more. When dealing with massive datasets that would be too big for human analysts to handle, AI-generated insights are very helpful. AI manages complexity and size, freeing up people to focus on communication, strategy, and interpretation. Businesses and their clients benefit from quicker analysis, better decisions, and more significant results when automation and human judgment are balanced.

2.6 GENERATING CLIENT-READY REPORTS WITH AI

Report creation is one of the most difficult phases in survey-driven and insight-based businesses. It takes a lot of time and work to turn those discoveries into a polished, client-ready report, even after data has been cleaned and insights have been found. Teams frequently have trouble keeping a consistent tone, organizing material, and making sure reports live up to client expectations. This procedure is altered by practical AI, which turns unstructured insights into reports that are prepared for delivery and review. Report generation powered by AI does not eliminate human intervention. Rather, it removes the most time-consuming and repetitive steps from the process, freeing up experts to concentrate on accuracy, strategic interpretation, and refining.

From Insights to Structured Reports

The process of writing a report usually starts with a blank document. Analysts have to choose how to arrange data, which portions to include, and how to clearly convey insights. Particularly when teams are working under strict schedules, this initial setup alone might take hours. By automatically transforming insights into a structured report format, AI streamlines this process. AI can arrange insights into conventional sections like an executive summary, significant findings, suggestions, and supporting explanations whenever they are ready.

Figure 2.3: AI-generated structured survey report prepared for client delivery.

A seamless transition from high-level ideas to in-depth observations is ensured by the content's logical arrangement. Clarity and consistency are brought about by this methodical approach. Each report has a standard format that makes it simpler for consumers to read and comprehend the results. This constancy becomes a significant benefit for companies that provide regular reporting, such weekly or monthly surveys. Teams don't have to change the report structure for every project, and clients are aware of what to anticipate.

Reducing Effort without Compromising Quality

Quality is a prevalent issue with reports produced by AI. Many experts are concerned that automated content can sound shallow or generic. In reality, AI-generated drafts are more of a solid foundation than a finished result. Teams receive a well-structured draft that already contains pertinent insights and concise explanations rather than having to write the full report by hand. After that, human reviewers intervene to confirm correctness, modify phrasing, and add context as necessary. Compared to writing everything from scratch, this review-focused workflow is significantly more effective. AI also aids in preserving linguistic coherence among reports. Team members' varying writing styles frequently result in inconsistent quality. AI-generated drafts offer a standard tone that reviewers can modify to suit client preferences. Professional quality is ensured without undue effort because to this harmony between automation and human refinement.

Customizing Reports for Client Expectations

Each client has different expectations in terms of presentation, tone, and depth. While some demand in-depth explanations and narratives based on evidence, others prefer succinct summaries. Reports produced by AI can be tailored to satisfy these requirements without requiring repetitive manual labor. Teams can direct AI to generate reports that meet particular client needs by modifying instructions and templates. For instance, a highly formal executive summary can be required by one customer, but a more conversational tone might be preferred by another. AI swiftly adjusts to these choices, enabling teams to effectively deliver customized reports. In this phase, human reviewers are essential. They make sure that suggestions are reasonable, language is suitable, and delicate information is conveyed with care. AI and human knowledge work together to provide reports that feel customized and deliberate rather than automated.

Impact on Time, Consistency, and Scalability

Time savings are the most obvious advantage of AI-driven report generation. A task that used to take days can now be finished in a few hours. Businesses are able to manage multiple projects at once and promptly address customer needs because to this quicker turnaround. Another significant benefit is consistency. AI reduces the variability brought on by hand drafting by applying the same standards and structure to all reports. With customers who depend on precise and repeatable insights, this consistency enhances brand reputation and fosters confidence.

When report generation is no longer a bottleneck, scalability is made possible. Without adding additional employees, small teams can handle more clients and bigger datasets. While humans concentrate on quality assurance and strategic interpretation, AI handles the increased workload. Businesses can transition from labor-intensive paperwork to a streamlined, review-driven process by incorporating AI into report preparation. AI is becoming a crucial partner in contemporary survey-driven operations since this change not only saves time but also improves the overall quality of client deliverables.

2.7 AUTOMATING WEEKLY AND MONTHLY SURVEY WORKFLOWS

Businesses that rely on surveys run on repetition. Weekly feedback is gathered, monthly customer satisfaction surveys are conducted, and larger research studies frequently adhere to quarterly cycles. This recurrent nature adds predictability, but it also adds a significant operational strain. Data downloads; response cleaning, theme analysis, insight extraction, and report preparation become repetitive tasks for teams. Over time, this repetition causes tiredness, delays delivery, and makes scaling challenging. This routine becomes a dependable, time-saving system when weekly and monthly survey workflows are automated with AI. Businesses can specify the workflow once and let AI carry it out automatically on a timetable, saving them from having to manually restart the process every cycle. This method increases capacity, speed, and consistency without requiring more workers.

The Nature of Recurring Survey Work

The majority of survey-based programs adhere to a set format. Stakeholders anticipate reports on particular dates, feedback is received on a regular basis, and the deliverables' format is essentially unaltered. Many teams continue to rely on physical labor for each cycle in spite of this regularity. Each time, analysts download files, clean datasets, apply the same analysis logic, and rewrite comparable summaries. Avoidable delays result from this manual repetition. Teams rush through tasks when deadlines are tight, which raises the possibility of mistakes or missed insights. Variations in report quality can also result from different team members' inconsistent handling. By standardizing work practices and guaranteeing that every cycle adheres to the same excellent procedure, automation solves these issues.

Designing an Automated Survey Workflow

Clarity is the first step towards automation. Each step of the survey process must be precisely defined in order to create a successful AI-driven workflow. The procedure is initiated with data collection, which is followed by automatic cleaning to eliminate redundant and insufficient responses. After the dataset is ready, AI uses preset logic to identify themes and extract insights. Creating a structured report that meets customer expectations is the last step. AI can carry out these procedures sequentially without human assistance when they are clearly mapped. Here, scheduling is crucial. Monthly reports can be produced at the conclusion of each month, quarterly studies can adhere to set calendar dates, and weekly surveys can be processed every Friday night. The team's responsibilities change from execution to review, concentrating solely on validation and improvement as opposed to tedious processing.

From Manual Effort to Scheduled Execution

Timing is one of the main benefits of automation. Workflows that are automated are independent of an individual's availability or workload. They operate continuously and dependably once planned. This guarantees that reports are consistently prepared on schedule, even in times of high demand or staffing shortages. Teams experience less stress when tasks are completed on time. Analysts don't have to rush to meet deadlines because they are confident that drafts will be available when needed. Planning is enhanced by this predictability, which enables companies to safely commit to supply schedules. The timely delivery of information in a recognizable, standardized format benefits clients as well.

Consistency and Quality at Scale

In survey-based work, consistency is essential. Customers anticipate similar insights from various reporting periods. Automation guarantees that the same themes, rules, and analysis techniques are used consistently. This increases the validity of insights and lessens variance brought on by personal perception. The number of surveys rises as companies expand. Under this stress, manual operations falter and frequently need more workers to keep up. Teams can manage increased volumes without corresponding increases in effort thanks to automated workflows. Scaling is both feasible and economical because AI can analyze larger datasets with the same speed and accuracy.

Human Review as a Control Layer

Automation does not eliminate the necessity for human intervention. Rather, it relocates people to crucial control locations. Team members check outputs for correctness, context, and relevance when AI completes the workflow. They guarantee that recommendations make sense for the client and that insights are in line with corporate objectives. Compared to manual processing, this review-focused position is more effective and less taxing. Instead of working on mechanical chores, analysts spend their time using their judgment and knowledge. As a result, higher-quality work is produced with less effort.

Business Impact of Automated Survey Workflows

Automating weekly and monthly survey routines has both strategic and operational implications. Businesses are able to take on more projects or provide faster delivery because turnaround time is much reduced. Long-term partnerships are strengthened and client trust is increased by consistent excellence. Teams are less likely to burn out, which boosts morale and retention. Above all, automation increases capacity. Teams can concentrate on more in-depth analysis, creative thinking, and advising responsibilities when mundane tasks are automated. Survey-driven companies become insight partners rather than data processors, adding more value without hiring more people. Organizations develop a sustainable growth model by automating routine survey procedures. AI turns into a reliable engine that operates in the background, making every reporting cycle quicker, cleaner, and more reliable than the previous one.

2.8 IMPLEMENTING AI IN A LIVE SURVEY BUSINESS

It takes more than just choosing the appropriate tool to implement AI in a real survey business. It necessitates a careful strategy that honors data realities, customer expectations, and current workflows. Many companies make the error of trying a complete transition all at once, only to run into misunderstandings, opposition, or inconsistent outcomes. Starting with a single, clearly defined survey project and progressively expanding as confidence and clarity increase is the most efficient method to implement AI. The venues used for live surveys are dynamic. Accuracy is crucial, customer deadlines are stringent, and data is constantly arriving. AI must therefore be implemented cautiously and in a way that enhances rather than interferes with current operations. When AI is used gradually, it becomes a dependable helper that enhances rather than overwhelms the company.

Starting with One Real Survey Workflow

Selecting the appropriate beginning point is essential for the effective adoption of AI. Rather than implementing AI in every project, companies could choose a recurrent survey process that the team is accustomed to. This could be a monthly employee engagement study, a weekly customer feedback survey, or a typical market research report sent to several clients. Comparing AI-assisted findings with conventional outputs is made simpler and less unclear by familiarity. AI should only be added to one or two phases of a workflow after it has been chosen. For instance, a team might start by summarizing open-ended responses or cleaning survey data using AI. Working with actual data instantly reveals AI's advantages and disadvantages.

Teams may see how successfully AI manages uneven language, spelling mistakes, and different response durations. This real-world experience is significantly more important than using ideal or fake datasets to test AI. Human supervision is still crucial during this stage. Team members should carefully examine AI outputs in order to comprehend its behavior rather than pass harsh judgment on it. Patterns appear fast. While some suggestions could yield obvious insights, others might need to be refined. This process of learning lessens anxiety or an excessive dependence on automation while increasing internal knowledge.

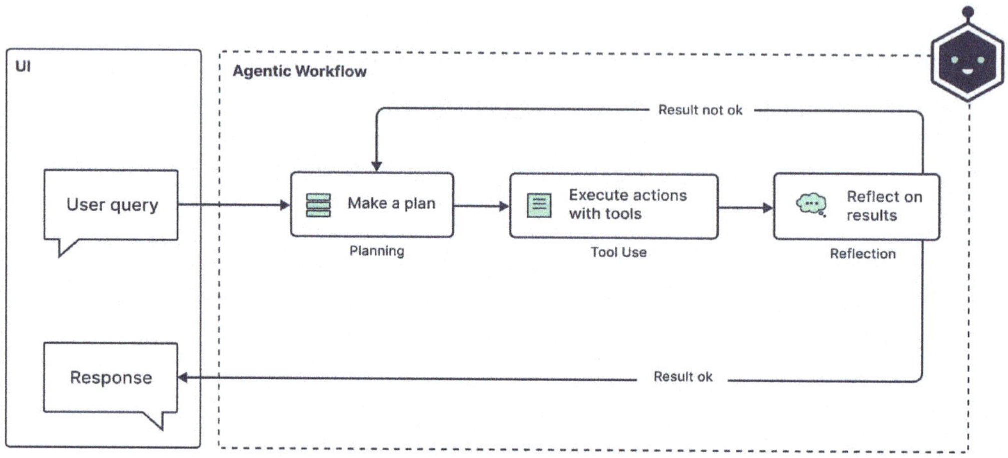

Figure 2.4: End-to-end AI-assisted workflow implemented in a live survey-driven business.

Source: *(Prajwal Yadav, 2025)*

Refining Processes and Building Confidence Gradually

Refinement becomes a natural part of the process when AI is evaluated on real-time survey data. Analysis rules can be changed to better suit business requirements, prompts can be made clearer, and review checkpoints can be established to guarantee quality. At this point, dependability is more important than speed. Every minor advancement boosts confidence in AI-generated results. It is very crucial to define review checkpoints. Before outcomes proceed, these checkpoints identify the situations in which human judgment is necessary. For instance, AI might be permitted to compile responses and create summaries, but before insights are shared with clients, a human analyst must approve them. This equilibrium guarantees responsibility and safeguards the organization's reputation.

Confidence increases with time. Members of the team start to recognize which jobs are best handled by AI and which need human involvement. Because of its clarity, AI may be used for a wider range of tasks, such creating preliminary reports or spotting patterns in several surveys. Scaling seems like a sensible next step rather than a dangerous leap because the team has already verified AI performance on smaller projects. Additionally, gradual deployment fosters client trust. Customers will see improvements in speed, consistency, and clarity even though they may not need to understand every technical aspect of AI usage. Adoption of AI improves long-term partnerships when it produces greater results without causing obvious disturbance.

Expanding AI Usage across Projects and Clients

Expansion becomes simpler once AI is shown to be dependable within a particular workflow. The setup time for new projects can be decreased by applying the same updated prompts and procedures to comparable surveys. Standardization increases productivity while preserving customizability. At this point, AI becomes a vital operational tool rather than just an experiment. Without hiring more employees, teams may manage bigger datasets, take on more clients, and produce insights more quickly. Crucially, because this progress is based on experience rather than presumptions, it seems controlled. AI is seen by successful survey companies as a dynamic system.

As data volume and customer expectations vary, they keep an eye on performance, modify workflows, and improve review procedures. This kind of thinking guarantees that AI adoption is both sustainable and in line with corporate objectives. AI implementation in a live survey company is not about abrupt change. It is about creating mechanisms that improve human competence, learning via practical application, and making continuous progress. AI may be a reliable partner that boosts quality and efficiency in survey-driven enterprises when it is implemented carefully and progressively.

A. SHORT QUESTIONS

1. What is meant by a survey-driven business?
2. Why manual survey data processing is considered inefficient?
3. How does AI help in cleaning survey data?
4. What role does AI play in identifying themes in survey responses?
5. Explain the importance of data preparation in survey analysis.
6. How does AI reduce human errors in survey processing?
7. What is meant by client-ready survey reports?
8. How can AI help in handling large volumes of survey responses?
9. Why is consistency important in survey reporting?
10. How does AI reduce workload and fatigue in survey-based businesses?

B. LONG QUESTIONS

1. Explain how AI can automate the complete workflow of a survey-driven business.
2. Describe the role of AI in cleaning and preparing survey data.
3. Discuss how AI helps in identifying themes and extracting insights from survey responses.
4. Explain the process of generating client-ready reports using AI.
5. Analyze the benefits of using AI in survey-driven businesses compared to manual methods.

C. MULTIPLE CHOICE QUESTIONS (MCQS)

1. Survey-driven businesses mainly deal with:

   a) Manufacturing data　　**b)** Financial records
   c) Feedback and responses　　**d)** Inventory data

2. Which stage of survey work is most time-consuming when done manually?

   a) Data storage　　**b)** Data cleaning
   c) Report printing　　**d)** Client meetings

3. AI helps in survey data preparation by:

   a) Increasing manual work　　**b)** Ignoring incomplete data
   c) Cleaning and validating responses　　**d)** Reducing data size randomly

4. Theme identification in survey analysis means:

   a) Designing questionnaires　　**b)** Grouping similar responses
   c) Collecting responses　　**d)** Printing reports

5. Which of the following is a benefit of AI-based survey analysis?

   a) Higher error rate　　**b)** Slower processing
   c) Improved consistency　　**d)** Increased workload

6. Client-ready reports generated by AI usually include:

   a) Raw data only　　**b)** Random responses
   c) Structured insights and summaries　　**d)** Unorganized information

7. AI reduces human fatigue mainly by:

   a) Increasing complexity　　**b)** Automating repetitive tasks
   c) Eliminating review steps　　**d)** Ignoring data quality

8. Which data format is commonly used for survey responses?

a) Video files **b)** Audio recordings
c) CSV or spreadsheet files **d)** Image files

9. Why is human review still important in AI-assisted survey workflows?

a) AI cannot read data **b)** AI outputs need validation
c) AI replaces analysts **d)** AI works without instructions

10. The biggest advantage of automating survey workflows using AI is:

a) Increased project delays **b)** Reduced insight quality
c) Faster and more reliable results **d)** Higher operational costs

CHAPTER 3

AI FOR EDUCATIONAL INSTITUTIONS

3.1 CHALLENGES FACED BY TEACHERS AND ADMINISTRATORS

Although they are the foundation of any educational institution, teachers and administrators are responsible for much more than just teaching in the classroom. Teachers are under increasing pressure to strike a balance between academic delivery and administrative responsibilities, regardless of the size of the institution. There is never enough time, there are frequently a lot of students, and parents, administrators, and school boards have increasingly high expectations.

These difficulties lead to a workplace where teachers believe that crucial facets of instruction and student involvement are neglected despite being continuously occupied. Lack of dedication or expertise is not the main problem. The majority of teachers have a strong desire for their pupils to succeed. The amount of time-consuming and repetitive work associated with teaching is the issue. A large amount of the working day is devoted to planning, testing, documentation, and communication, leaving little time for introspection, creativity, or individualized student care.

Growing Workload beyond the Classroom

Repeated lesson planning is one of the most enduring problems teachers encounter. Lesson plans need to be created, revised, and in line with evolving academic requirements, even while teaching the same subject or grade level year after year. This approach requires considerable consideration and time, particularly if educators wish to make their teachings interesting and pertinent. Repetition of lesson planning on a monthly or daily basis turns it from a creative exercise into a significant cognitive burden. Another level of pressure is added when assignments are created. In order to accommodate varying learning levels within the same classroom, teachers are frequently required to create various versions of assignments. This strategy greatly lengthens the preparation period even though it promotes inclusive education. Formal timetables seldom recognize the labor required to provide a variety of questions, worksheets, and exams.

Feedback and assessment add to the workload. It takes more than just marking correct or incorrect answers to check notebooks, assignments, and exam papers. It takes focus, clarity, and consistency to provide meaningful feedback. It can take hours to write personalized notes for each student, especially in large classes. This eventually causes tiredness, which might have an impact on feedback quality and speed. Attention must also be paid to administrative duties. Teachers and administrators are responsible for keeping track of attendance, documenting grades, keeping an eye on students' development, and preparing reports for internal or external authorities. Errors and duplication are more likely since a large portion of this activity is still done by hand or using disjointed systems. Although these duties are necessary, they make teachers feel more like data managers than mentors.

Impact on Student Interaction and Teaching Quality

The biggest effect of these difficulties is the decrease of face-to-face communication with students. Teachers' enthusiasm for direct engagement decreases when they spend evenings and weekends preparing materials or doing administrative tasks. Even though these encounters have a significant impact on student motivation and learning results, one-on-one chats, individualized assistance, and informal mentoring are frequently neglected. Similar demands are placed on administrators. Constant attention is needed to prepare institutional reports, manage staff tasks, coordinate schedules, and react to parent inquiries. Strategic planning and long-term improvement projects are hence frequently postponed.

Instead of directing the institution's future course, administrators become reactive rather than proactive, attending to urgent needs.Stress and burnout are the result of the accumulation. Teachers may believe that their labor never really ends, regardless of how hard they work. Reduced job satisfaction and, in certain situations, disengagement from the profession may result from this. Therefore, the task is profoundly human as well as operational. At this point, AI starts to have a significant impact. AI frees up instructors' time and mental space by taking care of preparation, organization, and tedious documentation activities in the background. Teachers and administrators can once again concentrate on what really matters teaching, learning, and helping kids as individuals when mundane work is eliminated.

3.2 AI-ASSISTED LESSON PLANNING

Although it is one of the most time-consuming aspects of teaching, lesson planning has long been a major duty for educators. Teachers must choose what to teach, how to teach it, and how to assess students' comprehension of the subject before they enter the classroom. This procedure necessitates careful consideration, adherence to curriculum requirements, and modification for the needs of the students. Lesson planning can become taxing and limit teachers' time for innovative instruction and student engagement when it is done regularly for several classes or subjects.

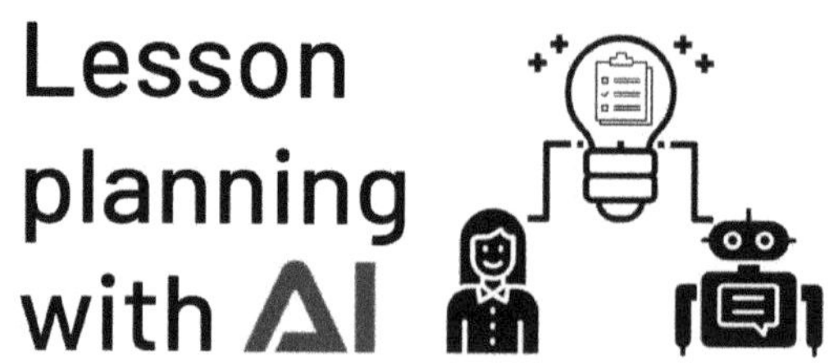

Figure 3.1: AI-assisted lesson planning process for teachers and academic staff.

AI-assisted lesson planning provides a workable solution to lessen this load without sacrificing the caliber of instruction. Teachers can focus on improving and customizing well-designed drafts rather than starting from scratch when using AI as a planning support tool. This modification increases consistency, saves time, and frees up teachers to devote more time to classroom engagement.

How AI Supports the Lesson Planning Process

When given straightforward and uncomplicated data, AI performs best in lesson preparation. Basic details like the grade level, subject, topic, and learning objectives are usually given by a teacher. AI can create an organized lesson plan that adheres to a logical teaching flow based on this input. Teachers are given a ready-made framework with all the necessary elements of a successful lesson in place of a blank page.

A typical AI-generated lesson plan may include:

- Clear learning objectives aligned with the topic
- An introduction or warm-up activity
- Step-by-step teaching activities
- Real-life examples or explanations
- Practice or discussion ideas
- Assessment or evaluation suggestions

Teachers have a solid foundation thanks to this arrangement. The plan offers guidance and clarity, but it does not specify how the course should be taught. Instructors are still allowed to alter exercises, incorporate their own teaching methods, or change the tempo in response to student feedback. AI also aids in preserving curricular standard alignment. AI can guarantee that exercises and evaluations stay on course when learning objectives are clearly stated. This lessens the possibility that teachers would stray from the standards of the syllabus, particularly when they are pressed for time.

Saving Time without Losing Teacher Control

Time efficiency is one of the main benefits of lesson planning with AI assistance. Teachers frequently devote hours to lesson planning, particularly when introducing new subjects or creating thorough plans for assessments or inspections. By taking care of the preliminary drafting, AI drastically cuts down on this preparation time. Teachers can focus on examining and improving the content rather of worrying about organization, sequencing, and language. Compared to beginning from scratch, this review-based method feels less taxing. Additionally, it enhances lesson consistency, particularly in establishments where several instructors teach the same subject or grade.

Teacher judgment is not replaced by AI. The realities of the classroom change every day. Each group has different levels of focus, prior knowledge, and learning pace. Teachers modify AI-generated plans to fit their pupils based on their experience. This harmony guarantees that lesson planning is both technologically assisted and human-centered. Reduced mental weariness is another significant advantage. Teachers have reduced stress and more motivation when planning is less monotonous. This beneficial impact frequently manifests in the way lessons are taught in the classroom, making them more interesting and well-structured.

Consistency and Flexibility in Teaching

In schools with multiple sections of the same class or set learning goals, teaching consistency is particularly crucial. AI facilitates the creation of consistent lesson plans while maintaining flexibility. The same AI-generated basic plan can be modified by teachers to suit their teaching preferences or the demands of the classroom.

This approach is particularly useful for:

- New teachers who need guidance on lesson structure
- Substitute teachers who require quick lesson outlines
- Coordinators who want aligned teaching across sections

Long-term planning is also supported by AI. Lesson plans that follow a logical flow of subjects can be created by teachers on a weekly or monthly basis. This prevents last-minute planning and preserves continuity. Flexibility is maintained at the same time. Instructors can modify course scheduling, add enrichment activities for advanced students, or simplify activities for slower learners. AI offers structure rather than rigidity. In the end, lesson planning with AI support improves instruction. It eliminates needless work while maintaining the teacher's function as a decision-maker and learning facilitator. Lesson preparation becomes quicker, more reliable, and more focused on what really counts effective learning in the classroom by fusing AI efficiency with human comprehension.

3.3 ASSIGNMENT AND WORKSHEET CREATION USING AI

Although making worksheets and assignments is a crucial component of teaching, it is also one of the most cognitively taxing jobs for teachers. Instructors must create questions that fit students' skill levels, support learning objectives, and hold students' attention throughout time. It takes a lot of mental energy to repeat this process on a weekly or even daily basis. Over time, exhaustion, a decrease in variety, and needless tension might result from the creative effort needed to constantly create new assignments. Practical AI offers a way to ease this burden while preserving the teacher’s control and educational intent.

By producing ready-to-use academic content based on precisely defined inputs, AI streamlines the preparation of assignments and worksheets. AI may create organized questions and activities that closely match classroom objectives when a teacher supplies parameters like subject, topic, grade level, and learning objectives. Teachers receive a draft that may be examined, improved, and modified to meet the requirements of their pupils rather than beginning with a blank page. As a result, the teacher's duty shifts from producing content continuously to carefully choosing and assessing it.

Reducing Cognitive Load in Assignment Design

Creating assignments that work entails juggling a number of variables at once. Questions should span a range of difficulty levels, be in line with curricular objectives, and assess comprehension rather than memory. Teachers who do this frequently experience a significant cognitive strain, particularly when they oversee several classes or disciplines. By managing the initial development of academic content, AI lessens this mental pressure. Teachers can select the most appropriate question type from a range of options that are connected to the same subject. AI lowers the possibility of misalignment by ensuring that worksheet content is aligned with learning objectives.

When several instructors teach the same subject or when organizations want to uphold consistent academic standards, this consistency is very beneficial. AI frees up teachers' mental capacity for more important work by handling the tedious parts of content creation. Teachers can concentrate on analyzing student replies, finding learning gaps, and developing focused interventions rather than devoting hours to formulating questions. Both work satisfaction and teaching quality are enhanced by this change.

Adapting Assignments to Different Learning Levels

In today's schools, accommodating a range of learning styles is one of the biggest problems. Teachers frequently have little time to produce various copies of the same project, despite the fact that students develop at varying rates. AI closes this gap by simplifying the creation of unique content. Teachers can request assignments with different levels of difficulty when utilizing AI. A single subject can be divided into more difficult issues for advanced students and easier practice exercises for struggling students. This flexibility promotes inclusive education without appreciably adding to the workload of teachers.

AI-generated content offers a versatile platform that educators can modify in response to the reality of the classroom. AI facilitates reinforcement and revision as well. For pupils who require more practice, teachers can create extra worksheets without creating new content from start. This guarantees fast and reliable learning help. As a result, teachers are better able to address each student's unique needs and pupils receive more individualized academic help. Time efficiency is another significant advantage.

Teachers can devote more time to assessing students' comprehension rather than creating content when assignments and worksheets are produced rapidly. Learning results take precedence over administrative preparation in assessment. This enhances the teaching-learning process as a whole. The importance of teachers in education is not eliminated by using AI to create assignments. Rather, it makes it stronger. Teachers are still in charge of choosing pertinent material, guaranteeing academic accuracy, and assisting students in their study. AI serves as a helpful tool that manages tedious design tasks, freeing up educators to concentrate on what really matters understanding students, enhancing education, and creating relevant learning opportunities.

3.4 SUPPORTING DIFFERENT LEARNING LEVELS

Every classroom has a variety of students with varying skills, passions, and rates of learning. While some students pick up concepts quickly and seek out new challenges, others require more time, practice, and assurance to absorb the same content. One of the most difficult tasks for educators is handling this diversity. Giving each student individualized attention becomes challenging when class time is limited and workloads are high. This is where useful AI can be helpful by assisting educators in better addressing various learning levels without adding to their workload. Although differentiated learning has long been regarded as the best strategy in education, its manual implementation necessitates a great deal of planning and preparation.

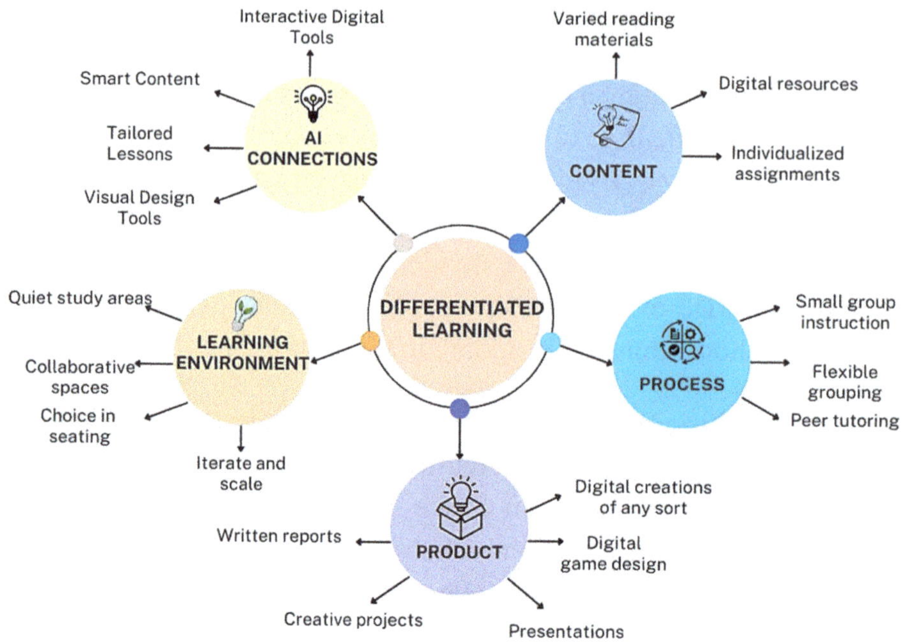

Figure 3.2: Use of AI to support students with different learning levels and abilities.

Source: *(Miguel Guhlin, 2024)*

Time limits make it challenging for teachers to modify tasks, offer more practice, or push advanced students. By assisting in the development of educational resources that cater to various student demands while maintaining teacher control over the learning process, AI helps close this gap.

Addressing Learning Diversity in the Classroom

Learning differences can take many different shapes in a regular classroom. Some students perform well at grade level, some struggle with basic ideas, and some advance quickly and lose interest when material seems repetitious. Slow learners may become frustrated and rapid learners may become bored if the same subject is taught to every student in the same manner. By providing additional worksheets, review sessions, or enrichment activities, teachers have always tried to manage this variability. However, it takes time to manually create many versions of the same assignment.

Additionally, it adds to the teacher's workload, which frequently results in burnout or inconsistent support. AI makes this process easier by creating several learning resources based on the same fundamental idea. AI can produce easier exercises for students who need more help and more difficult issues for those who need more challenge when a teacher gives them a topic and learning aim. This frees up the teacher to concentrate on teaching and mentoring instead of creating content. Differentiated learning is transformed from an ideal that is challenging to execute into a workable plan with the use of AI. Instructors are able to react to students' requirements more rapidly and adaptably.

Using AI to Personalize Practice and Revision

The ability of AI to customize practice and revision is one of its most significant contributions to enabling various learning levels. Students that struggle frequently require repeated exposure to concepts in various contexts. AI can create extra practice questions, detailed explanations, and review exercises for particular subjects that students struggle with. AI can recommend extracurricular activities for advanced students. These could be application-based inquiries, higher-order puzzles, or exploratory exercises that promote more in-depth thought. Giving quick learners these kinds of chances keeps them interested and involved without forcing the teacher to arrange lessons separately.

Teachers can find learning gaps with the help of AI. AI can identify trends in student performance data, such as often misinterpreted subjects or mistakes. This information can subsequently be used by teachers to organize focused revision sessions or give particular students specialized assistance. This data-driven strategy guarantees that instructional efforts are in line with real learning needs and increases accuracy. Consistency is another significant benefit. It is more difficult to provide consistent support for all pupils when teachers are worn out or under stress. AI-generated resources adhere to predetermined guidelines and frameworks, guaranteeing that every student receives practice that is suitable for their learning objectives.

Reducing Teacher Workload While Improving Learning Outcomes

Teachers frequently worry that personalized learning adds to their workload. This is a legitimate issue in the absence of support. AI, however, modifies the situation by lowering the time and effort needed to produce unique elements. Teachers can use AI-generated drafts and make necessary revisions instead of creating numerous worksheets or revision activities by hand. This drastically cuts down on preparation time, freeing up teachers to focus more on student engagement, clarification, and support. By eliminating tedious duties, AI enhances rather than replaces the job of the teacher. AI promotes inclusive education as well. When they need more assistance, students are often reluctant to ask for it. Teachers may quietly offer guidance through AI-generated individualized practice, which lowers stigma and boosts student confidence. At the same time, advanced students are given challenging assignments that acknowledge their skills.

This well-rounded strategy eventually fosters a more encouraging learning atmosphere. Students stay involved, feel understood, and advance at their own speed. When they witness better learning outcomes without excessive workloads, teachers feel less stressed and more satisfied. One of the main challenges in education has always been providing support for varying learning levels. This problem is easier to handle with useful AI. AI enables educators to effectively address a variety of student requirements while maintaining the human connection at the core of teaching by supporting material production, practice customization, and performance analysis.

3.5 GRADING AND FEEDBACK ASSISTANCE

One of a teacher's most significant duties is grading students' work, but it also takes a lot of time. It frequently takes hours outside of class to review assignments, assess exam responses, and provide insightful feedback. Teachers find themselves making the same remarks and corrections over and over again as class sizes and assessment frequency rise. The amount of time available for student interaction, lesson development, and introspection is diminished by this repetitive effort.

By helping teachers with the grading and feedback process without interfering with their professional judgment, practical AI provides significant support in this area.Giving computers control is not the goal of AI-based grading aid. It is about maintaining the teacher's position as the ultimate authority while utilizing technology to lessen physical labor. When applied properly, AI becomes a helpful tool that enables educators to work more productively and give students higher-quality feedback.

Reducing the Burden of Manual Grading

It takes constant focus to grade by hand. Instructors must carefully examine each response, compare it to the expected responses, point out any errors, and determine how to effectively convey any improvements. Fatigue inevitably develops when dozens or hundreds of pupils go through this process again. This may eventually result in inconsistent feedback, brief remarks, or a delay in the return of tasks. AI can help by analyzing student responses and identifying trends throughout the class. AI examines responses collectively rather than evaluating each input separately. It can determine which questions the majority of students answered poorly, which ideas are frequently misinterpreted, and which pupils routinely receive worse grades. Before they start their in-depth evaluation, teachers are given a clear picture by this collective analysis.

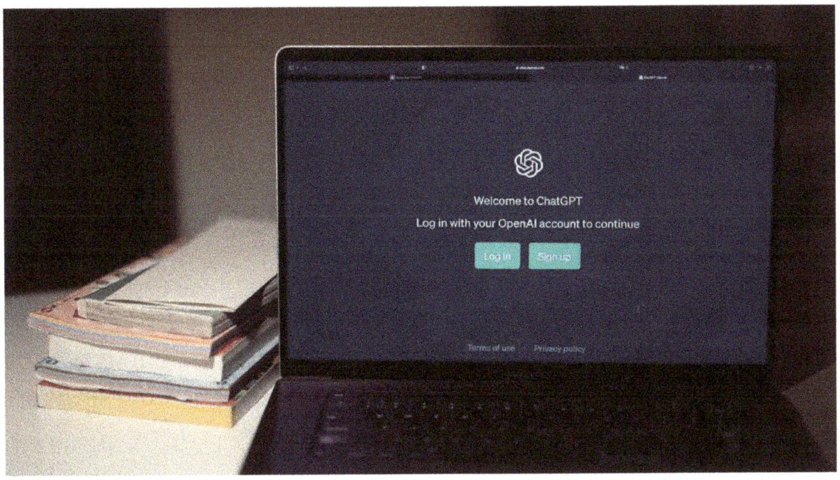

Figure 3.3: AI-assisted grading and feedback generation supporting teachers' evaluation tasks.

Based on patterns found, AI can also create preliminary feedback statements. For instance, AI might recommend a feedback explanation that explains the problem clearly if a lot of students have trouble with the same subject. Teachers can then modify this recommendation to fit their classroom setting and teaching methodology. This method guarantees that feedback is considered and pertinent while saving time. Crucially, AI does not determine final grades or assess students' comprehension. It merely arranges data so that teachers may work more quickly and reliably.

Improving Feedback Quality and Consistency

Giving constructive criticism is crucial for learning. Feedback that is timely targeted at improvement rather than punishment is most beneficial to students. Writing this kind of criticism on a regular basis, however, can be difficult, particularly when time is of the essence. AI assists by guaranteeing uniformity in feedback. AI-generated recommendations retain a consistent explanation when comparable errors occur, lowering the possibility of conflicting messages. This consistency makes the evaluation process more equitable and aids students in better understanding expectations.

Additionally, AI enables educators to go beyond superficial remarks. AI promotes more insightful feedback by spotting deeper patterns, like recurrent misconceptions across tasks or tests. Instead of focusing on specific symptoms, educators can address the underlying reasons. For example, feedback can concentrate on conceptual clarity rather than individual mistakes if students frequently apply a formula incorrectly or misunderstand a concept. Speed is an additional benefit. Students receive instruction while the subject matter is still fresh in their thoughts thanks to faster feedback. This keeps pupils interested and enhances learning results. As a result, teachers are less stressed about deadlines and grading backlogs.

Preserving Teacher Judgment and Human Connection

Preserving teacher judgment is one of the most crucial features of AI-assisted grading. AI is unable to comprehend the emotions, learning challenges, or personal development of students. Instructors do. AI should never take the place of teachers in making decisions because of this. AI serves as a preliminary aid instead. Data is arranged, trends are highlighted, and potential feedback is drafted; nonetheless, everything is reviewed and finalized by the teacher. This guarantees that feedback stays sympathetic, context-aware, and consistent with the values of the classroom. Depending on the needs of each particular student, teachers may decide to provide encouragement, personalize remarks, or change the tone.

By relieving teachers of tedious mechanical tasks, AI preserves this human connection rather than eliminating it. Reflective teaching is also supported by AI-assisted grading. AI assists teachers in identifying places where instruction may need to be adjusted by displaying trends across student performance. Both educators and students gain from this feedback loop, which enhances the educational process as a whole. One of the most beneficial uses of useful AI in education is grading and feedback support, as the needs of education continue to rise. When applied properly, AI lessens burden, enhances the quality of feedback, and assists educators without undermining their authority or expertise.

3.6 TRACKING STUDENT PERFORMANCE WITH AI

Despite being one of the most crucial duties in education, monitoring student performance is frequently overlooked. Although the realities of daily workload makes it challenging to practice consistently, teachers and administrators are generally aware that ongoing monitoring leads to higher learning results. Assignment records stay dispersed, test papers accumulate, and attendance data is only examined when issues are apparent. Performance tracking consequently shifts from being proactive to being reactive. This is altered by practical AI, which makes performance monitoring ongoing, controllable, and significant.

Figure 3.4: Analysis and tracking of student performance using AI-driven tools.

AI does not add to the workload for teachers. Rather, it arranges current scholarly data in a manner that facilitates prompt decision-making. AI gives a more comprehensive view of students' development over time by combining test data, assignment outcomes, and attendance trends. This enables teachers to concentrate on deeper learning trends rather than just surface-level evaluation.

From Isolated Records to Continuous Performance Insight

Performance data is incomplete in typical classroom settings. Assignments are examined individually, test results are kept in registers, and attendance is noted separately. Even though each record is valuable on its own, it becomes challenging to make connections between them and comprehend overall progress. By combining all academic markers and analyzing them as a single dataset, AI closes this gap. AI searches for patterns rather than individual outcomes when analyzing student performance data. It can determine whether a kid with poor test scores also exhibits inconsistent attendance or unfinished tasks.

In a similar vein, it might draw attention to pupils who excel academically but gradually lose interest. It is challenging to manually get this level of insight, particularly in large classes. For teachers, this means less guesswork. Instead of relying on memory or occasional reviews, they can access structured performance summaries that reflect both short-term and long-term progress. Performance tracking becomes a natural part of teaching rather than an additional responsibility.

Supporting Early Intervention and Targeted Teaching

Early detection is one of the biggest benefits of AI-driven performance tracking. Learning gaps may occur gradually and go undetected until test results show an issue. Students may already be having difficulties or losing confidence by that point. By spotting weak points as they appear, AI helps stop this. AI can identify subjects where several students are performing poorly by examining test results and assignment trends. This enables educators to go over ideas again before the gaps get bigger. AI can monitor how a student's performance varies between classes or themes at the individual level, which makes it simpler to determine where assistance is required.

Better remedial planning is supported by this realization. Teachers can create focused interventions based on real data rather than holding general revising sessions. Teaching time is used more effectively, and students receive targeted support. This method eventually boosts students' confidence and academic achievement. Additionally, AI assists teachers in distributing attention throughout the classroom. While struggling pupils get the most of the attention, strong performers are sometimes disregarded since they seem self-sufficient. By keeping an eye on advanced students, performance tracking enables teachers to offer enrichment activities as needed.

This well-rounded strategy promotes inclusive education. Because AI does the heavy job, performance tracking becomes ongoing rather than sporadic. Every time fresh findings are added, data is automatically examined. Teachers can evaluate students' progress without waiting until the conclusion of the term. Rather, they can watch trends emerge and react instantly. The way educators engage with data is altered by this ongoing visibility. Performance records transform from static papers into dynamic instruments that inform day-to-day choices.

Learning gets more individualized and instruction becomes more responsive. AI frees up teachers' time to concentrate on pupils by lowering the administrative work needed to evaluate performance data. It turns tracking from a neglected chore into an effective support system. When applied carefully, AI improves the relationship between instructional strategies and learning objectives, increasing the adaptability and efficacy of education.

3.7 COMMUNICATI ON WITH PARENTS USING AI

A healthy learning environment depends on parents and schools having effective communication. Parents anticipate meetings, significant announcements, future events, and frequent updates regarding their child's development. However, drafting these messages on a regular basis becomes a laborious and mentally taxing work for educators and administrators. Every message needs to be precise, courteous, professional, and individualized enough to feel significant. It gets harder to keep this equilibrium as workloads rise. A dependable method of streamlining parent communication while maintaining the human touch necessary for schooling is provided by practical AI.

Figure 3.5: AI-supported communication between educational institutions and parents.

Source: *(Michelle Connolly, 2023)*

In terms of communication, AI does not take the place of educators or administrators. Rather, it helps them by creating organized drafts that minimize repetitious work and save time. Instead of having to start from scratch every time, educators can concentrate on reviewing, personalizing, and enhancing the message because AI takes care of the initial writing.

Reducing the Burden of Repetitive Communication

Communication with parents in the majority of educational institutions follows standard procedures. Exam notices, meeting reminders, weekly newsletters, progress summaries, and event announcements frequently reiterate similar material with just little modifications.

Every time, writing these notes by hand takes up time that could be used for planning, teaching, or helping students. AI assists by producing well-organized drafts based on basic inputs like the message's goal, the class or grade level, and important elements to include.

For instance, AI can create a fair message that emphasizes behavior, attendance, academic performance, and areas for development when creating a monthly progress report. After that, teachers can modify their language to fit the needs of certain pupils or classroom situations. Writing tiredness is much reduced by this method. Teachers examine and improve AI-generated manuscripts rather than writing messages line by line. Particularly during hectic times like exams, parent-teacher conferences, or school functions, the procedure becomes quicker and less stressful.

Maintaining Clarity, Professionalism, and Trust

Tone is one of the main obstacles to parent-child communication. Messages should be clear, kind, and encouraging without coming across as overly formal or informal. Confusion or needless worry might result from poor communication. AI lowers the possibility of badly phrased messages by assisting in maintaining a consistent professional tone throughout all contacts. AI-generated texts are particularly helpful when communicating delicate topics like behavioral comments or progress problems. AI assists teachers in avoiding emotionally charged language by delivering facts in a cool, collected manner. In order to make parents feel informed rather than condemned, teachers can then tailor the message with empathy and context.

Another important factor in fostering trust is consistency. Parents feel more a part of the school when they receive timely and organized communication. By making sure that crucial information is not overlooked and that messages adhere to a standard format across many departments and courses, AI promotes uniformity. Language help is an additional benefit. AI can help prepare translations or create communications in plain, uncomplicated language in schools where parents have different linguistic backgrounds. This increases accessibility and guarantees that all families receive good communication.

Supporting Teachers and Administrators without Losing the Human Touch

Fear of losing a personal connection is a prevalent worry when employing AI in communication. But rather than serving as a final voice, AI functions best as a drafting helper. Administrators and teachers continue to have complete discretion over what is sent. Before any message is sent to parents, it is reviewed, customized, and approved. This human evaluation process guarantees that the communication reflects both the educator's comprehension of each student and the school's values. Humans provide warmth, context, and judgment; AI manages structure and clarity. Teachers can communicate more frequently and effectively without feeling overburdened because to this relationship.

AI eventually assists organizations in creating standard communication templates that align with their expectations and culture. These templates guarantee that communication quality is high even when teams shift and facilitate the onboarding of new employees. Automation for its own sake is not the goal of using AI for parent communication. It's about making room for better connections. AI frees up educators to concentrate on meaningful contact, thoughtful comments, and prompt responses by relieving them of the stress of repetitious writing. When applied properly, AI enhances communication rather than replaces it, making parent involvement in regular classroom activities more reliable, professional, and controllable.

A. SHORT QUESTIONS

1. What is the role of AI in educational institutions?
2. Why do teachers face workload challenges in modern education systems?
3. How does AI assist in lesson planning for teachers?
4. What is meant by AI-assisted assignment creation?
5. How can AI support differentiate learning in classrooms?
6. Explain how AI helps in grading and feedback assistance.
7. Why is student performance tracking important in education?
8. How does AI help in identifying learning gaps among students?
9. What role does AI play in communication with parents?
10. How does AI reduce administrative workload in educational institutions?

B. LONG QUESTIONS

1. Explain how AI supports teachers in lesson planning, assignment creation, and classroom management.
2. Discuss the role of AI in grading, feedback generation, and student performance analysis.
3. Describe how AI can be used to support students with different learning levels.
4. Explain the benefits of using AI for communication and administrative tasks in educational institutions.
5. Analyze how AI improves efficiency and effectiveness in teaching and learning processes.

C. MULTIPLE CHOICE QUESTIONS (MCQS)

1. One of the main challenges faced by teachers is:

   a) Lack of students **b)** Excessive administrative work
   c) Too much free time **d)** Lack of classrooms

2. AI-assisted lesson planning mainly helps teachers by:

   a) Replacing teachers **b)** Reducing preparation time
   c) Eliminating teaching **d)** Increasing workload

3. Differentiated learning refers to:

   a) Teaching only top students
   b) Same assignments for all students
   c) Supporting students with different learning needs
   d) Ignoring slow learners

4. AI can help in grading by:

   a) Making final decisions independently **b)** Highlighting common mistakes
   c) Ignoring student answers **d)** Increasing bias

5. Student performance tracking using AI helps in:

   a) Punishing students **b)** Identifying strengths and weaknesses
   c) Reducing assessments **d)** Eliminating exams

6. AI-generated feedback is useful because it is:

   a) Random **b)** Time-consuming
   c) Consistent and structured **d)** Always perfect

7. Communication with parents using AI mainly involves:

   a) Automated punishment notices **b)** Drafting messages and reports
   c) Conducting parent meetings **d)** Student discipline

8. Which task can AI automate in education?

   a) Teaching values **b)** Lesson planning
   c) Classroom discipline **d)** Student emotions

9. AI in education is best described as:

   a) A replacement for teachers **b)** A support tool for educators
   c) A threat to learning **d)** A temporary trend

10. The biggest benefit of using AI in education is:

a) Increased complexity
b) Reduced teacher involvement
c) Improved efficiency and time management
d) Elimination of human judgment

CHAPTER 4

AI FOR SMALL TECH TEAMS

4.1 WORKING INSIDE A SMALL TECH TEAM

Small tech teams function in a quick-transferring and demanding environment. Not like massive businesses wherein roles are really separated, small groups rely upon flexibility. An unmarried team member regularly takes on a couple of duties at some stage in the day. A developer may additionally start the morning writing code, spend midday reviewing pull requests, handle client-pronounced issues in the afternoon, and replace documentation before the day ends. Even as this adaptability continues teams agile, it additionally creates consistent context switching that reduces awareness and increases the chance of mistakes.

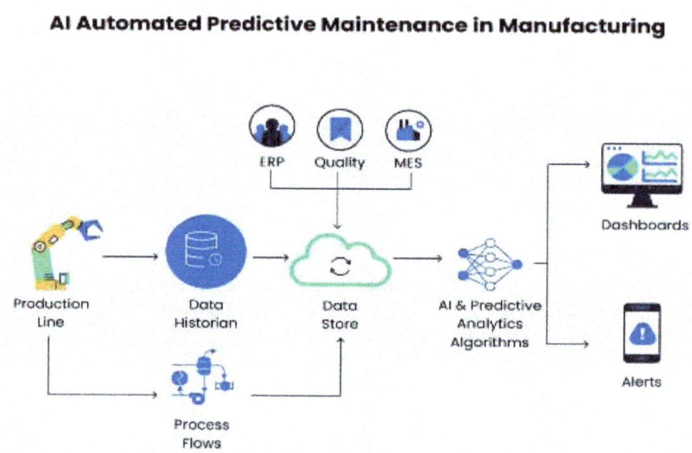

Figure 4.1: AI-supported workflow enabling small tech teams.

Source: *(Liz Lockhart Lance, 2022)*

In such environments, productiveness is not restricted by means of technical talent but through intellectual overload. Every venture shift calls for the brain to reorient, keep in mind details, and adapt to a brand new sort of thinking. Through the years, this consistent switching drains energy and slows development. Sensible AI offers a manner to lessen this cognitive burden by way of supporting the maximum repetitive and textual content-heavy elements of a developer's workload, allowing small teams to characteristic greater efficiently without increasing headcount.

The reality of Multitasking in Small Tech teams

Multitasking is often visible as a power in small tech groups, but in practice it comes with hidden prices. Writing code requires deep awareness, at the same time as responding to assist tickets demands a special mind-set targeted on conversation and trouble explanation. Documentation work, then again, requires readability, structure, and attention to detail. While developers flow swiftly between those obligations, their attention will become fragmented. This fragmentation affects pleasant. Code written underneath frequent interruptions is more likely to contain insects.

Documentation up to date hastily may also lack readability. Support responses written under pressure can leave out crucial context. Over time, these small excellent issues accumulate and create technical debt, client dissatisfaction, and internal frustration. AI helps deal with this hassle through absorbing much of the routine cognitive load. Obligations that contain summarizing information, drafting popular text, or converting one form of content material into another are especially well desirable for AI support. By using delegating those obligations to AI, builders can maintain consciousness for work that genuinely calls for human judgment and creativity.

How AI Supports Focus and Workflow Continuity

AI acts as a stabilizing layer inside the everyday workflow of a small tech crew. Instead of continuously moving between obligations, team individuals can rely on AI to prepare first drafts and based outputs which might be prepared for overview. This adjustments the character of labor from constant creation to controlled refinement. For instance, when a developer finishes imposing a function, AI can generate a draft description for documentation based on code remarks or dedicate messages. The developer only wishes to study and alter the textual content, in place of write it from scratch. Similarly, whilst aid tickets arrive, AI can summarize the difficulty, extract key information, and advocate a reaction framework.

This lets in developers to address problems quickly without breaking their awareness for long periods.AI also facilitates preserve consistency across crew outputs. In small teams, one of kind humans may additionally write documentation or launch notes in unique styles. AI-generated drafts provide a constant baseline, making communique clearer for customers and inner stakeholders. Consistency reduces confusion and saves time at some stage in opinions. Every other critical benefit is decreased intellectual fatigue. Textual content-heavy duties together with writing reasons, summaries, or reviews are draining when repeated daily. AI handles this repetition effortlessly, allowing human group participants to preserve intellectual energy for complicated problem-fixing. This stability improves both productiveness and job satisfaction.

Improving Collaboration without adding Complexity

Small tech groups depend closely on collaboration, however limited time frequently restricts effective verbal exchange. AI supports collaboration through organizing and clarifying data earlier than it reaches human hands. Assembly notes can be summarized, selections may be documented definitely, and action gadgets can be based robotically. This guarantees that everyone stays aligned without lengthy observe-up discussions. AI also enables new or much less skilled group participant's ramp up faster.

By means of summarizing present documentation, past choices, and machine behavior, AI reduces the dependency on senior developers for primary explanations. This makes knowledge more available and reduces interruptions. Importantly, AI does now not replace the collaborative nature of small teams. As an alternative, it strengthens it by using getting rid of friction. Conversations turn out to be extra focused, critiques come to be quicker, and misunderstandings are reduced. Teams spend much less time explaining context and greater time constructing solutions.

Balancing Automation and Human manipulate

Even as AI gives valuable aid, successful teams hold clear obstacles. AI prepares drafts, summaries, and guidelines; however human beings stay liable for final selections. This balance guarantees accuracy, responsibility, and alignment with mission dreams. Small tech teams advantage maximum whilst AI is dealt with as an assistant as opposed to an expert. Builders evaluate AI-generated outputs, practice area know-how, and make final adjustments. This method builds consider in AI systems whilst retaining professional judgment.

Over time, as groups come to be acquainted with AI behavior, they discover ways to manual it greater successfully. Activates improve, workflows stabilize, and outputs come to be more and more reliable. This sluggish getting to know technique ensures that AI integration feels natural in preference to disruptive. Working inside a small tech group calls for consistent version, cognizance, and collaboration. Via taking over repetitive and text-heavy tasks, AI reduces intellectual overload and permits builders to concentrate on significant work. In preference to juggling countless duties, group individuals advantage respiration area to suppose definitely, write higher code, and supply higher-high-quality products. On this manner, AI turns into no longer just a tool, however a sensible accomplice inside the each day lifestyles of a small tech crew.

4.2 HANDLING REQUIREMENTS AND FEATURE REQUESTS

In small tech teams, dealing with requirements and function requests is one of the most crucial but difficult duties. New thoughts, computer virus reviews, and development tips arrive constantly from exclusive directions. Clients ship emails, users submit comments through apps, assist groups increase tickets, and internal discussions generate additional requests. Every supply makes use of its own language and degree of element, making it hard to create a clear and unified knowledge of what sincerely needs to be built.

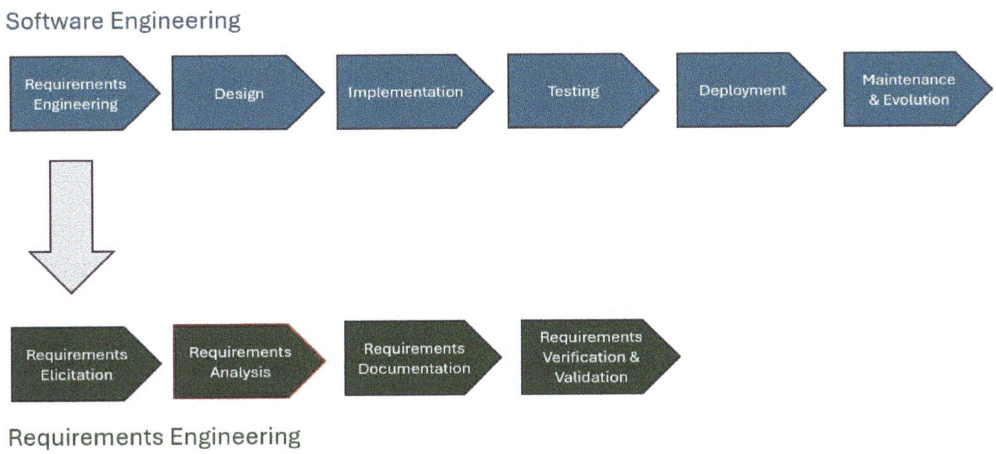

Figure 4.2: AI-assisted conversion of feature requests.

While this information is treated manually, teams spend a big quantity of time just organizing inputs. Developers and product managers must examine lengthy electronic mail threads, scan chat messages, interpret vague feedback, and convert all of it into actionable requirements. This technique not handiest slows improvement however also will increase the chance of misunderstandings. Practical AI presents a based manner to manage this complexity and flip scattered statistics into clear, usable necessities.

From Scattered Inputs to based requirements

One in every of the most important troubles in requirement dealing with is fragmentation. Feature requests hardly ever arrive in an easy, structured layout. A customer might describe a hassle emotionally, a help ticket may additionally focus handiest on signs, and an internal dialogue may additionally anticipate shared context that is not documented. While these inputs are exceeded directly to builders, confusion is almost inevitable. AI helps through performing as a smart interpreter. It is able to read raw inputs from multiple assets and extract the core intent behind every request.

In preference to forcing team contributors to manually summarize lengthy messages, AI converts unstructured textual content into established requirement descriptions. It identifies what the user wants, why they want it, and what final results they expect. This dependent view gives the team a clean starting point for dialogue and making plans. Another primary benefit is consistency. Human-written necessities often vary in style and readability depending on who organized them. AI-generated summaries comply with a consistent structure, making it less difficult for everybody to study and apprehend them. While necessities are supplied in a uniform way, decision-making becomes faster and much less at risk of misinterpretation.

Clarifying expectancies and lowering Ambiguity

Ambiguity is one of the major causes of wasted improvement attempt. While expectations are unclear, builders may construct features that technically paintings but do no longer solve the real problem. Solving those troubles later consumes time beyond regulation and assets. AI reduces ambiguity by means of highlighting key expectations embedded inside feature requests. It is able to pick out useful wishes, implied priorities, and capability constraints referred to within the enter. For instance, if a consumer emphasizes ease of use or pace, AI can surface these as vital expectations.

This enables the crew understand not just what wishes to be built, however how it should behave from the user's perspective. AI additionally allows groups stumble on missing records early. When a request lacks clarity, AI-generated summaries frequently make gaps more visible. This lets in groups to ask centered follow-up questions in place of engaging in long, unfocused discussions. Clean questions lead to quicker answers, which in turn accelerate development.

Saving Time and Improving Team Communication

Managing requirements manually frequently leads to repeated discussions. One-of-a-kind team contributors interpret the identical request in another way, resulting in conferences that awareness more on clarification than on actual planning. AI streamlines communication by way of providing a shared reference point that everybody cans assessment. When requirements are summarized virtually at the start, developers, designers, and stakeholders perform with the same knowledge. This alignment reduces again-and-forth communication and minimizes rework.

Development time is used more efficaciously due to the fact groups begin constructing with self-belief as opposed to assumptions. AI additionally supports documentation. Established requirements generated by means of AI may be saved and reused, creating a clean report of why sure capabilities were constructed. This documentation becomes precious when onboarding new team members or revisiting selections later. Instead of counting on memory or scattered messages, teams have a reliable source of reality.

Assisting quicker and smarter development selections

Clean necessities at once impact development speed and excellent. While teams recognize what desires to be constructed from the start, they could estimate attempt more accurately and plan sprints greater effectively. AI-generated requirement summaries provide a strong foundation for prioritization, helping teams decide which capabilities ought to be addressed first. AI does not update human judgment in decision-making. As an alternative, it enhances it by way of providing records in a way that is simpler to evaluate. Product managers can consciousness on strategic choices in preference to administrative cleanup. Developers can concentrate on implementation instead of interpretation.

Through the years, the use of AI in requirement managing leads to extra predictable workflows. Teams expand self-belief of their planning process because misunderstandings lower and effects improve. This stability is specifically treasured for small tech teams that have to supply outcomes with limited assets. Using AI to address requirements and characteristic requests transforms a historically messy technique right into a dependent and efficient one. By means of changing raw inputs into clean requirements, highlighting expectancies, and decreasing ambiguity, AI allows teams shop time, avoid mistakes, and build higher merchandise with more confidence.

4.3 AI SUPPORT FOR CODING AND DEVELOPMENT

Artificial intelligence has end up an increasingly important help machine in cutting-edge software improvement. In recent years, developers have moved past viewing AI as a futuristic idea and began the use of it as a realistic assistant for the duration of every day coding tasks. In preference to replacing human programmers, AI now works alongside them, assisting accelerate development at the same time as keeping first-class and control. This shift has modified how small and big development teams method coding, trying out, and preservation.

One of the maximum sizeable ways AI helps coding is thru the technology of boilerplate code. Writing repetitive structures inclusive of primary functions, records models, configuration files, or trendy utility additives consumes a huge quantity of developer time. These elements are important but rarely intellectually difficult. AI can generate these structures fast primarily based on simple instructions, allowing builders to transport at once to the parts of the assignment that require deeper questioning and creativity. This reduces fatigue and prevents builders from spending precious strength on routine styles.

Figure 4.3: AI providing coding assistance.

AI also assists in suggesting logical systems at some point of improvement. Whilst developers describe what a chunk of software ought to do, AI can suggest viable strategies, algorithms, or manage flows that healthy the requirement. Those hints act as beginning points instead of final solutions. Builders examine the common sense, regulate it if necessary, and combine it into the larger device. This collaborative method shortens the time required to transport from idea to implementation at the same time as preserving humans firmly in price of decision-making. Any other essential contribution of AI is its capability to identify capacity errors early in the development technique. AI equipment can assessment code as it's far written and highlights issues consisting of syntax errors, inefficient good judgment, or lacking aspect instances.

Catching those problems early prevents them from spreading via the codebase and decreases the time spent on debugging later. Even as AI does not update thorough testing or code reviews, it offers a further layer of aid that improves standard reliability. Regardless of those benefits, AI does not eliminate the need for professional builders. Structure design, system scalability, overall performance optimization, and safety selections continue to be firmly inside human duty. These regions require contextual knowledge, enjoy, and judgment that AI cannot completely mirror. Builders determine how unique components interact, how records flow through systems, and a way to defend applications from vulnerabilities. AI helps these efforts but does now not direct them. The connection between builders and AI works pleasant while simply defined roles are maintained.

AI handles repetitive styles, indicates options, and hurries up ordinary tasks. Developers compare outputs, refine good judgment, and make sure that solutions align with project desires and technical requirements. This stability prevents overreliance on automation at the same time as maximizing efficiency. AI assist also allows improve gaining knowledge of and skill improvement within teams. Junior developers can use AI-generated guidelines to recognize coding patterns and satisfactory practices extra quick. Instead of looking through documentation or suffering with syntax, they receive contextual steering that helps them progress faster. Senior builders gain through spending much less time answering repetitive questions and greater time focusing on complicated layout demanding situations. This creates a more healthy gaining knowledge of surroundings without compromising code exceptional.

Another advantage of AI-assisted development is consistency. When AI is used to generate not unusual systems and patterns, codebases turn out to be extra uniform. Consistent code is easier to hold, review, and amplify. Groups spend less time deciphering distinct patterns and greater time improving functionality. Over time, this consistency reduces technical debt and improves lengthy-time period venture balance.AI also helps rapid iteration. Development often includes experimenting with distinct processes before settling on the best solution. AI makes this experimentation faster by means of fast generating options. Developers can take a look at thoughts, discard what does not work, and refine what does, all without excessive manual attempt. This pliability encourages innovation even as preserving development timelines underneath control.

Importantly, AI does not eliminate duty. Builders continue to be responsible for the very last code that is deployed. They overview AI-generated outputs, check them very well, and make certain compliance with protection and performance requirements. This duty reinforces the idea that AI is a device, now not a choice-maker. When used responsibly, it strengthens expert practice in place of weakening it. The collaboration among developer and AI in the end improves speed without sacrificing first-rate.

Initiatives circulate forward faster because repetitive work is automated and cognitive load is reduced. At the identical time, human oversight ensures that systems continue to be sturdy, comfy, and aligned with actual-global needs. This partnership allows small groups to compete with larger companies and enables developers to focus on fixing meaningful issues as opposed to repetitive duties. As AI keeps adapting, its function in coding and improvement will probably expand. But, its price will usually depend on how thoughtfully its miles included into human workflows. Whilst builders treat AI as a supportive assistant in place of an alternative, they unencumber better productiveness, higher gaining knowledge of, and extra sustainable improvement practices.

4.4 DOCUMENTATION AND KNOWLEDGE MANAGEMENT

Documentation is a vital part of any company's lengthy-time period fulfillment, but in small groups it's far often handled as a low priority. Tight time limits, restricted manpower, and regular strain updated supply effects push documentation up to date up-to-date of the task list. Team participants rely upon quick chats, emails, or private memory up to date keeps work moving. Over time, this creates a delicate gadget where essential knowledge exists most effective in scattered conversations or in the minds of some people. While a person leaves the crew or takes a wreck, treasured records are lost, and productivity suffers.

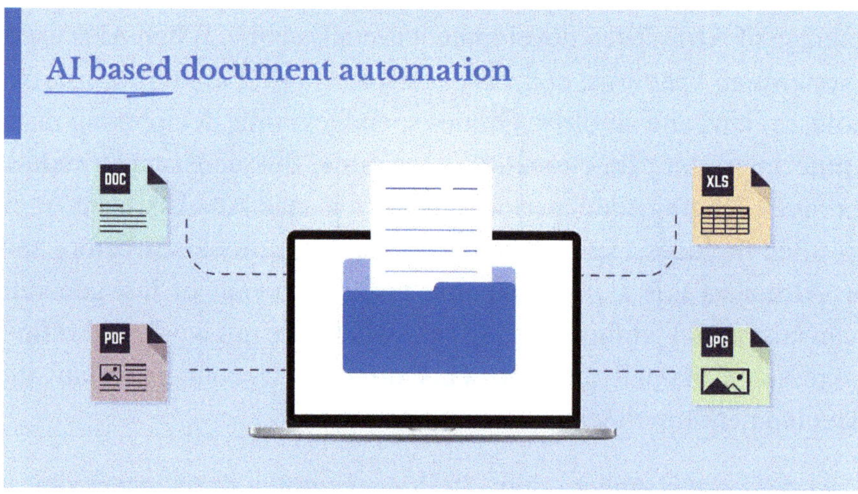

Figure 4.4: Automation of technical documentation.

Source: *(Pankaj Tripathi, 2025)*

In small teams, documentation normally fails now not up to date humans do now not recognize its significance, but due up updated preserving it looks like greater work. Writing unique files after finishing responsibilities calls for time and cognizance that groups experience they cannot spare. As initiatives grow, the distance between real machine conduct and written documentation widens. New crew contributors battle up to date recognize processes, existing individuals waste time answering the same questions repeatedly, and selection-making slows down up to date updated lack of readability. That is where sensible AI up to date a powerful guide machine. AI does no longer require teams up to date up to date prevent running and start documenting one after the other. As a substitute, it captures information from work this is already being finished and transforms it in updated based, usable documentation.

By way of integrating AI in up-to-date day by day workflows, documentation up to date updated a byproduct of labor up to date a further duty. One of the maximum treasured contributions of AI is its capability up-to-date code remarks in up-to-date meaningful documentation. Developers often write brief comments up-to-date provide an explanation for logic or highlight essential sections of code. In my opinion, these remarks are useful; however they're hardly ever prepared right into a coherent rationalization of ways a device works. AI can study via codebases and comments and generate clear documentation that explains functionality, dependencies, and utilization in easy language. This allows teams up-to-date maintain technical documentation without manually rewriting facts. AI additionally performs a vital function in coping with knowledge generated at some point of conferences. In small groups, conferences frequently manifest often and informally. Decisions are made quickly, thoughts are exchanged, and movement faceup updated are mentioned. Regrettably, those discussions are rarely documented nicely.

Notes may be incomplete, or they'll be saved updated in personal notebooks or chat messages which are up to date updated up-to-date retrieve later. AI can method assembly notes or transcripts and convert them in up-to-date structured summaries that spotlight key choices, duties, and subsequent steps. This guarantees that crucial facts do not disappear as soon as the assembly ends. Some other place wherein AI provides good sized cost is transforming characteristic descriptions in up-to-date consumer publications. Product features are frequently discussed in technical phrases that make sense up-to-date developers however not updated sup updated up to datemersupdated. Writing user documentation requires translating this technical language in up to date clear commands, which takes time and careful effort. AI can bridge this hole by way of reading feature descriptions, necessities, or internal notes and generating consumer-pleasant publications.

These drafts can then be reviewed and subtle by means of the group earlier than being shared with up-to-date.

AI-driven documentation and knowledge management bring several practical advantages to small teams:

- Documentation stays aligned with actual work because it is generated from real inputs such as code, notes, and descriptions
- Knowledge becomes centralized instead of scattered across multiple tools and conversations
- New team members can onboard faster with access to clear, updated information
- Existing team members spend less time explaining repeated concepts
- The risk of knowledge loss is reduced when people leave or change roles

Another vital gain is consistency. While documentation is written manually by way of exclusive human beings, tone, structure, and degree of detail often vary. AI-generated documentation follows consistent styles and formats, making it simpler to examine and understand. This consistency improves usability and decreases confusion, especially in developing groups wherein a couple of people make contributions to the equal task. AI also allows preserve documentation updated. In small groups, outdated documentation is frequently worse than no documentation at all. People prevent trusting documents after they understand information is not accurate. Because AI can regenerate documentation quickly each time modifications occur, groups can update expertise bases frequently without beginning from scratch. This keeps documentation relevant and dependable.

Expertise management is not only about storing information but also approximately making it reachable. AI can assist prepare documentation through categorizing content, generating summaries, and highlighting key sections. This makes it less complicated for team participants to find what they need once they want it. Rather than looking through long files or chat histories, human beings can access clean, based information quickly. From a psychological perspective, AI reduces resistance to documentation. When documentation feels computerized and convenient, teams are more likely to simply accept it as a part of their workflow. Humans no longer see it as a further burden however as a natural outcome in their work. This cultural shift is crucial for lengthy-term understanding sustainability.

AI does not replace human judgment in documentation. Groups still need to check outputs, make sure accuracy, and regulate language when essential. However, the heavy lifting is executed by means of AI, allowing humans to consciousness on validation in place of creation. This balance guarantees nice without overwhelming the crew. In small groups, in which each hour counts, AI-powered documentation and information control create stability. Work turns into much less dependent on individual memory and extra reliant on shared know-how. As tasks grow and evolve, this shared know-how base supports continuity, efficiency, and confidence. Practical AI transforms documentation from an omitted challenge right into a strategic asset, assisting small groups paintings smarter, communicate higher, and scale without chaos.

4.5 TEST CASE AND BUG REPORT GENERATION

Software program testing is one of the maximum essential ranges inside the improvement lifecycle, yet its miles often the maximum time-ingesting and underneath-resourced. Small tech groups, in particular, struggle to stability characteristic development with thorough trying out. Tight time limits, restrained manpower, and common modifications in necessities make it difficult to design comprehensive check instances and maintain clean computer virus documentation. As an end result, testing is on occasion rushed, increasing the hazard of defects attaining manufacturing.

Realistic AI offers meaningful help on this location with the aid of assisting groups with take a look at case technology and computer virus report summarization. In preference to replacing testers or developers, AI strengthens their work via improving coverage, clarity, and velocity. Whilst used efficiently, AI turns into a dependable testing assistant that helps groups keep fine without slowing down transport.

The venture of manual testing in Small Tech groups

Guide test design calls for cautious thinking and deep knowledge of necessities. Testers ought to imagine how customers would possibly engage with the machine, identify possible failure factors, and don't forget unusual situations that might not be obvious. This cognitive effort becomes onerous while repeated across more than one features and releases. Worm reporting gives a similar project. Developers and testers frequently describe issues in unique methods, main to doubtful or incomplete bug reviews.

Essential details which include steps to reproduce, predicted conduct, and machine context may be missing. Poorly written malicious program reports slow down resolution and increase frustration in the crew. AI enables deal with those troubles through bringing shape and consistency to each checking out and bug documentation.

AI-Assisted check Case generation

AI can generate take a look at instances via analyzing necessities, consumer testimonies, and present system conduct. While given clear inputs, AI produces structured test thoughts that testers can assessment and refine. This approach extensively reduces the time spent brainstorming check eventualities.

AI-generated take a look at instances typically recognition on both expected behavior and ability failure situations. This guarantees that trying out goes past fundamental capability and explores how the device behaves under extraordinary situations.

AI supports test case generation by:

- Interpreting functional requirements and user stories
- Suggesting test scenarios based on typical user actions
- Identifying boundary conditions such as limits and constraints
- Highlighting areas where errors are likely to occur

Instead of starting from a blank document, testers receive a well-organized list of test ideas that can be adapted to project needs.

Improving Unit Testing with AI Support

Writing unit tests is frequently disregarded because of time constraints, despite the fact that unit testing is crucial for preserving code quality. Developers may put off testing in favor of concentrating on core logic, which would increase technical debt. AI helps developers by making suggestions for unit tests based on behavior and code structure. AI can suggest test scenarios that verify both normal operation and failure circumstances by examining functions, inputs, and outputs.

AI helps with unit testing by:

- Suggesting test cases for common input values
- Identifying edge conditions such as null values or empty inputs
- Highlighting scenarios where exceptions may occur
- Encouraging consistent testing practices across the codebase

This support makes unit testing less intimidating and more approachable, especially for small teams with limited testing expertise.

Identifying Edge Cases More Effectively

Edge cases are situations that don't happen often but can have major consequences if they're not handled correctly. Because they take more creativity and time, these cases are frequently missed during manual testing. Because AI systematically examines patterns and variations, it is excellent at spotting edge cases. Because it doesn't rely on presumptions or routines, it is less prone to overlook peculiar circumstances.

AI can suggest edge cases such as:

- Extremely large or small input values
- Unexpected user behavior
- Timing-related issues
- Data inconsistencies or formatting errors

By including these scenarios in testing, teams improve system robustness and reduce the likelihood of production failures.

AI-Driven Bug Report Summarization

Clear, succinct, and comprehensive bug reports are the most successful. Unfortunately, a lot of bug reports are poorly organized and written fast, which makes them hard to read. By extracting important details from unprocessed descriptions, logs, or user comments, AI may condense bug reports. It arranges this data in a format that is consistent and easy for developers to work with.

AI-assisted bug reporting improves clarity by:

- Summarizing the issue in simple language
- Highlighting steps to reproduce the problem
- Identifying expected versus actual behavior
- Including relevant system context

Clear bug reports reduce back-and-forth communication and speed up resolution.

Enhancing Test Coverage without Increasing Workload

Improved coverage without corresponding increases in effort is one of the main benefits of employing AI in testing. AI-generated test cases frequently highlight situations that human testers could miss because of time constraints.

Better test coverage leads to:

- Fewer production defects
- More stable releases
- Increased confidence during deployment

By assisting with test design and documentation, AI allows teams to test more thoroughly without extending timelines.

Maintaining Human Control and Judgment

AI is helpful, but human inspection is still necessary. To guarantee relevance and accuracy, testers and developers must verify AI-generated test cases and bug descriptions. Instead of being seen as an authority, AI should be seen as a collaborator. Understanding corporate context, setting priorities, and reaching final decisions all involve human skill. This equilibrium guarantees that AI improves quality without posing new dangers.

Integrating AI into Existing Testing Workflows

AI works best when integrated smoothly into existing processes. Teams do not need to redesign their testing strategy entirely. Instead, AI can be introduced gradually as a support tool.

Common integration points include:

- Test case brainstorming during sprint planning
- Unit test suggestions during development
- Bug summarization during issue triage

This gradual adoption helps teams build confidence and adapt workflows naturally.

Long-Term Benefits for Small Tech Teams

AI-assisted testing eventually results in better organized and reliable procedures. Teams improve their test design and documentation practices. By capturing knowledge more efficiently, reliance on individual team members is decreased. This stability is particularly helpful for small tech teams. Even when team composition shifts or workloads rise, AI aids in upholding quality standards. AI is essential to improving software quality while honoring the limitations of small development teams by facilitating the creation of test cases and the clarity of defect reports.

4.6 SPRINT PLANNING WITH AI ASSISTANCE

One of the most crucial and time-consuming tasks in agile development is sprint planning. During planning sessions, small tech teams frequently find it difficult to strike a balance between clarity and speed. Priorities change regularly, tasks come from a variety of sources, and dependencies aren't always immediately apparent. Sprint planning meetings can therefore become drawn out, unfocused, and psychologically taxing. By arranging material before the meeting starts, practical AI provides significant support in this area, freeing teams to focus on decision-making rather than preparation.

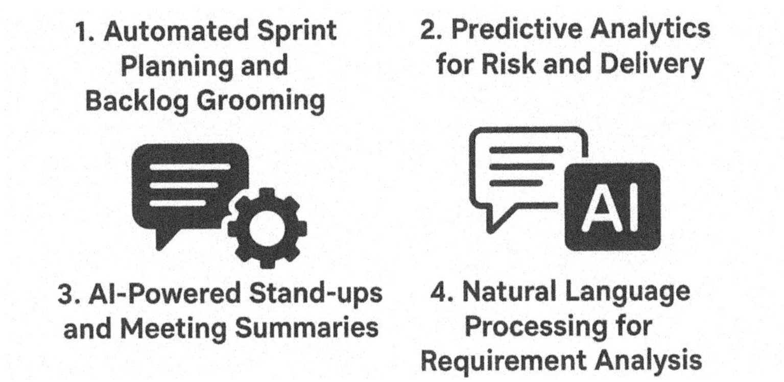

Figure 4.5: Use of AI in agile sprint planning.

Source: *(Jignesh Pabari, 2018)*

AI does not take the role of team judgment or sprint planning talks. Rather, it facilitates the process by taking care of the laborious task of organizing and summarizing data. When applied properly, AI turns sprint planning from an administrative task into a strategic dialogue.

The Challenges of Traditional Sprint Planning

Sprint planning often begins with dispersed information in small IT teams. Emails, chat messages, help tickets, and casual comments can all contain feature requests. Someone needs to gather these inputs, turn them into tasks, and create a backlog that the team may review before any prioritization can take place. Just this preparation takes up important time. Teams frequently spend excessive amounts of time reviewing task descriptions, defining each item, and attempting to recall task dependencies during the actual meeting. Incomplete or poorly formatted data makes estimation challenging. As a result, fundamental clarity takes precedence over priorities and dangers. Longer meetings and a lack of faith in sprint commitments result from this. AI addresses these challenges by preparing information in advance. When task data is clean, summarized, and structured, sprint planning becomes faster and more effective.

How AI Prepares Sprint Data before the Meeting

When it comes to processing vast amounts of text-based data, AI excels. It can read work descriptions, problem reports, and feature requests and turn them into succinct summaries. Without going into needless detail, these summaries convey the main points of the work. AI may examine the backlog and find related activities prior to sprint planning. Tasks that rely on the same element or functionality, for instance, can be grouped together. This facilitates teams' comprehension of the sprint's broad structure and how specific activities relate to more general objectives. Additionally, dependencies that might not be immediately apparent can be highlighted by AI. AI can identify linkages between jobs that depend on shared resources, approvals, or previous work. This early awareness increases planning accuracy and lessens surprises throughout development. By the time the sprint planning meeting begins, the team is already looking at a refined and organized view of upcoming work.

Improving Estimation and Prioritization

Uncertain task definitions frequently compromise accurate estimating, which is essential for effective sprints. By offering contextual information and consistent task summaries, AI enhances estimating. Teams are better able to estimate work when tasks are properly defined. By emphasizing elements like job urgency, the frequency of related issues, or alignment with release goals, AI can also aid with prioritization. AI offers a structured beginning point that lessens disagreement over fundamental facts, even while the team always has the final say on prioritizing. Sprint planning conversations may now concentrate on risks and trade-offs rather than clarification thanks to this capability. Teams can spend less time figuring out what each assignment truly entails and more time determining what matters most.

Making Sprint Planning Meetings Shorter and More Focused

Reduced meeting time is one of the most obvious advantages of AI-assisted sprint planning. Meetings proceed more quickly when information is prepared ahead of time. Teams no longer have to look for missing context or read lengthy work descriptions aloud. Decisions should not be made hastily in shorter meetings. Rather, they demonstrate improved readiness. When AI manages information organization, team members are prepared to talk about dependencies, priorities, and possible obstacles. Meetings that are focused also increase participation. When conversations are effective and relevant, developers and product owners are more likely to actively participate. Better alignment and a greater dedication to sprint objectives result from this.

Enhancing Collaboration and Transparency

AI-assisted sprint planning increases team transparency. Everyone has a common knowledge of the sprint scope when activities are arranged logically and dependencies are apparent. During implementation, this clarity lessens misunderstandings and enhances teamwork. Stakeholders outside the development team also gain from transparency. Communicating deadlines, progress, and risks to clients or management is made simpler with well-defined sprint plans. This communication can be supported by summaries produced by AI without the need for extra manual reporting. This transparency gradually fosters trust. Effective planning increases the likelihood of consistent delivery, boosting trust in the process and the individuals involved.

Supporting Continuous Improvement in Agile Teams

Planning a sprint is a continuous process. As teams grow and learn, it changes. AI facilitates this evolution by simplifying the analysis of previous sprints. AI can assist teams in finding trends and opportunities for improvement by examining finished projects, delays, and modifications. Teams are able to continuously improve their planning strategy thanks to this feedback loop. Sprint planning becomes increasingly practical, predictable, and capacity-aligned over time. Teams are encouraged to concentrate on improvement rather than battling fires by using AI-assisted sprint planning.

Teams may focus more on producing high-quality software when planning is clear and effective. Automation for its own sake is not the goal of sprint planning with AI support. The goal is to eliminate friction from a crucial procedure.By summarizing tasks, highlighting dependencies, and organizing work before discussions begin, AI enables teams to plan smarter, communicate better, and deliver more consistently.

4.7 RELEASE NOTES AND DEPLOYMENT SUPPORT

When a new product or upgrade is released, small tech teams frequently have the familiar but tiresome task of creating release notes. Release notes are essential for informing users, clients, and internal stakeholders about changes, even while development activity gets the majority of the attention. Unfortunately, this work is frequently put off until the last minute, monotonous, and time-consuming. Release remarks are so frequently hurried, inconsistent, or lacking. An efficient method of streamlining this procedure while enhancing consistency and clarity is offered by practical AI.

Release notes are more than a formality. They serve as the formal documentation of any modifications made to a product. They aid consumers with comprehending enhancements, problem fixes, and new features. Additionally, they provide correct information regarding upgrades to internal teams including operations, sales, and customer support. Release notes can lead to confusion and a rise in support inquiries when they are done incorrectly. When executed well, they foster transparency and confidence.

Why Release Notes Become a Bottleneck

Release notes are rarely someone's main duty in small IT teams. Product managers concentrate on delivery schedules, developers concentrate on coding, and testers concentrate on quality. The task of writing release notes is often neglected since it sits between these positions.

Several factors contribute to this bottleneck:

- Information about changes is scattered across commits, task boards, and messages
- Developers use technical language that is not user-friendly
- Repeated formatting is required for every release
- Tight deadlines leave little time for careful writing

Because of these challenges, release notes are often copied from previous versions and edited quickly, leading to inconsistent tone and structure across releases.

How AI Supports Release Note Generation

AI functions as an intelligent summarizer of development activity, making the preparation of release notes easier. To determine what has been delivered in a release, it can examine finished tasks, code commits, pull requests, and change logs. AI creates a structured draft that clearly emphasizes important changes based on this analysis. Teams are given a pre-made paper with pertinent sections and well-organized data rather to beginning from scratch. Then, instead of concentrating on creation, human reviewers may concentrate on improvement. The amount of work needed for each release is greatly decreased as a result. Additionally, AI-generated drafts guarantee that nothing crucial is overlooked. AI can record changes throughout the whole codebase when numerous developers contribute to a release, eliminating the need for individual memory or manual tracking.

Key Elements AI Can Capture Effectively

When generating release notes, AI is particularly effective at identifying and organizing information that already exists within development systems.

AI can reliably extract and summarize:

- New features introduced in the release
- Bug fixes and resolved issues
- Performance or stability improvements
- Minor enhancements and optimizations

By structuring this information clearly, AI helps team's present updates in a way that is easy for users to understand and for stakeholders to reference.

Improving Consistency across Releases

Consistency is one of the main benefits of employing AI for release notes. Tone and structure frequently change when release notes are prepared by multiple people by hand. Some releases could be too specific, while others might be too technical. By adhering to preset forms and linguistic patterns, AI aids in the standardization of release notes. Users will find it easier to scan and comprehend updates if all releases adhere to the same format. Additionally, professionalism and brand communication are strengthened by consistency. Teams can gradually adjust AI prompts to fit their intended tone formal, informal, or educational. Once perfected, it will be easy to keep the same style for all subsequent releases.

Supporting Deployment Communication

Deployment operations are strongly related to release notes. Many stakeholders require quick and accurate information after a release is deployed. This procedure is aided by AI-generated release notes, which facilitate quicker communication.

During deployment, AI-assisted notes help with:

- Informing users about new changes

- Updating internal teams such as support and sales
- Documenting release history for future reference

Because AI drafts are generated quickly, communication delays are reduced. Teams can align deployment announcements with actual release timing instead of sending updates late.

Reducing Developer and Manager Workload

Managers or developers must transition from technical work to writing while creating release notes by hand. This context change raises frustration and decreases productivity. By managing the initial drafting process, AI lessens this strain. While AI automatically gathers and summarizes their work, developers may concentrate on creating and improving features. Rather than gathering data from many sources, managers can examine and approve notes. The efficiency of the workflow is increased by this division of labor. As a result, the team as a whole experiences a more seamless and stress-free release preparation process.

Human Review and Final Control

AI can produce correct drafts, but human inspection is still crucial. AI lacks human comprehension of corporate priorities, consumer sentiment, and product strategy. Final review makes sure that release notes don't contain sensitive or superfluous information and are in line with communication objectives. When necessary, human reviewers may add contextual explanations, reorder sections, or change the phrasing. This partnership guarantees the accuracy and significance of release notes. A balanced approach that optimizes productivity without compromising quality is produced by combining AI drafting with human refinement.

Long-Term Benefits for Small Tech Teams

AI-assisted release note creation eventually integrates into a dependable deployment process. Teams devote more time to invention and improvement and less time to tedious documentation. Communication about releases becomes timely, professional, and predictable. This method scales organically as products expand and releases increase in frequency. Without requiring more human labor, AI adjusts to bigger codebases and more intricate change logs. This capacity is a major benefit for small tech teams with limited resources. AI turns release notes from an ongoing hassle into a reliable, efficient procedure that advances communication and development objectives.

4.8 ENDS-TO-END DEVELOPMENT WORKFLOW EXAMPLE

In a small tech group, each stage of development is intently connected. A function idea quickly turns into a task, then into code, testing, documentation, and in the end a launch. Whilst these stages are dealt with manually and independently, delays and inconsistencies regularly seem. A quit-to-give up improvement workflow supported by AI helps small groups keep pace, clarity, and great without increasing complexity. This situation illustrates how AI can guide the complete development lifecycle, from the instant a demand is acquired to the factor where the function is launched and communicated to customers. The focal point is not on changing builders, however on decreasing repetitive paintings and enhancing coordination throughout levels.

From Requirement consumption to development Readiness

The workflow begins when a new requirement enters the device. This may come from consumer feedback, inner discussions, aid tickets, or emails. In a traditional setup, group individuals manually study and interpret those inputs, frequently main to ambiguity or lacking information. AI simplifies this level through studying raw input and changing it right into a dependent requirement description. AI can summarize the request, spotlight key expectancies, and become aware of potential constraints. This dependent output allows developers and product managers to speedy understand what desires to be constructed. By using standardizing requirement interpretation, AI reduces misunderstandings and shortens the time spent clarifying scope.

Human evaluation guarantees that the summarized requirement as it should be displays consumer rationale before development starts off evolved. Once the requirement is permitted, AI assists in breaking it down into improvement-prepared responsibilities. It may advise challenge descriptions that include context, anticipated conduct, and simple acceptance criteria. Developers receive clearer responsibilities, which improves estimation accuracy and decreases rework for the duration of implementation.

Supporting Coding, Testing, and Release Activities

Throughout the coding segment, AI acts as an improvement assistant rather than a decision-maker. It allows generate boilerplate code, indicates common sense styles, and helps developers via decreasing repetitive typing. Developers continue to be fully accountable for architectural selections, safety issues, and overall performance optimization. AI without a doubt quickens execution by way of coping with routine coding styles. As development progresses, checking out becomes the next recognition. AI supports this level via suggesting test eventualities based on feature conduct and capability aspect instances. It can help summarize malicious program reports, making them less difficult to recognize and reproduce. This improves check insurance and guarantees that not unusual failure factors are addressed early. Human testers and builders validate these guidelines to maintain reliability. Documentation is often behind schedule or left out in small groups because of time constraints. AI integrates documentation into the workflow via changing improvement notes and code feedback into readable documentation drafts.

This guarantees that understanding is captured at the same time as the context is still clean. Builders can evaluation and refine documentation quick instead of writing it from scratch later. The very last degree of the workflow includes getting ready for launch. AI assists with the aid of analyzing completed obligations and generating draft release notes that specify changes in clear language. This protects time and ensures consistent communication with stakeholders and customers. Human evaluate ensures accuracy and suitable tone before ebook. A give up-to-end AI-assisted improvement workflow brings shape and continuity to small tech teams. Via helping each stage with sensible assistance, AI reduces friction and lets in groups to consciousness on problem-fixing and innovation. The end result is a smoother development procedure that gives you excellent outcomes without overwhelming constrained resources.

A. SHORT QUESTIONS

1. What is meant by a small tech team?
2. Why do small tech teams face workload pressure?
3. How does AI help in handling requirements and feature requests?
4. What role does AI play in task creation for tech teams?
5. How does AI assist developers during coding?
6. Explain the use of AI in technical documentation.
7. How does AI support testing and bug handling?
8. What is the role of AI in sprint planning?
9. How does AI help in generating release notes?
10. Why AI is considered a productivity multiplier for small tech teams?

B. LONG QUESTIONS

1. Explain how AI supports small tech teams throughout the software development lifecycle.

2. Describe the role of AI in requirement analysis and task management.
3. Discuss how AI assists in coding, documentation, and testing activities.
4. Explain the importance of AI in sprint planning and release management.
5. Analyze the benefits and limitations of using AI in small tech teams.

C. MULTIPLE CHOICE QUESTIONS (MCQS)

1. Small tech teams usually work with:

   a) Unlimited resources
   b) Large specialized departments
   c) Limited people and time
   d) No deadlines

2. AI helps in requirement handling mainly by:

   a) Ignoring user feedback
   b) Summarizing and structuring requests
   c) Writing final code automatically
   d) Eliminating planning

3. AI-assisted coding primarily helps developers by:

   a) Replacing developers
   b) Writing all logic without review
   c) Generating boilerplate and suggestions
   d) Increasing complexity

4. Documentation is often neglected in small teams because:

   a) It is unnecessary
   b) It requires no effort
   c) Time and resource constraints
   d) It is automated already

5. AI can help in testing by:

   a) Ignoring bugs
   b) Generating test cases
   c) Removing test requirements
   d) Avoiding quality checks

6. Sprint planning with AI becomes more effective because AI can:

   a) Replace team meetings
   b) Prioritize and summarize tasks
   c) Eliminate deadlines
   d) Remove human input

7. Release notes generated by AI are useful because they are:

   a) Random and informal
   b) Structured and consistent
   c) Unnecessary
   d) Difficult to understand

8. AI supports small tech teams mainly by:

a) Increasing workload **b)** Reducing productivity
c) Automating repetitive tasks **d)** Removing accountability

9. Which task is best suited for AI assistance in tech teams?

a) Strategic decision-making **b)** Writing boilerplate code
c) Ethical judgment **d)** Team motivation

10. AI in small tech teams should be used as:

a) A full replacement for humans **b)** A background experiment
c) A supportive productivity tool **d)** A risk to job security

CHAPTER 5

BUILDING AGENTIC AI WORKFLOWS

5.1 MOVING BEYOND SINGLE PROMPTS

Users are frequently exposed to artificial intelligence as a conversational tool. After typing a query or command, people get a response and proceed. Particularly for brief tasks like explanations, summaries, or idea generating, this contact feels natural and helpful. However, AI's potential is still constrained when applied just in this manner. Seldom does real organizing work take place in a single phase.

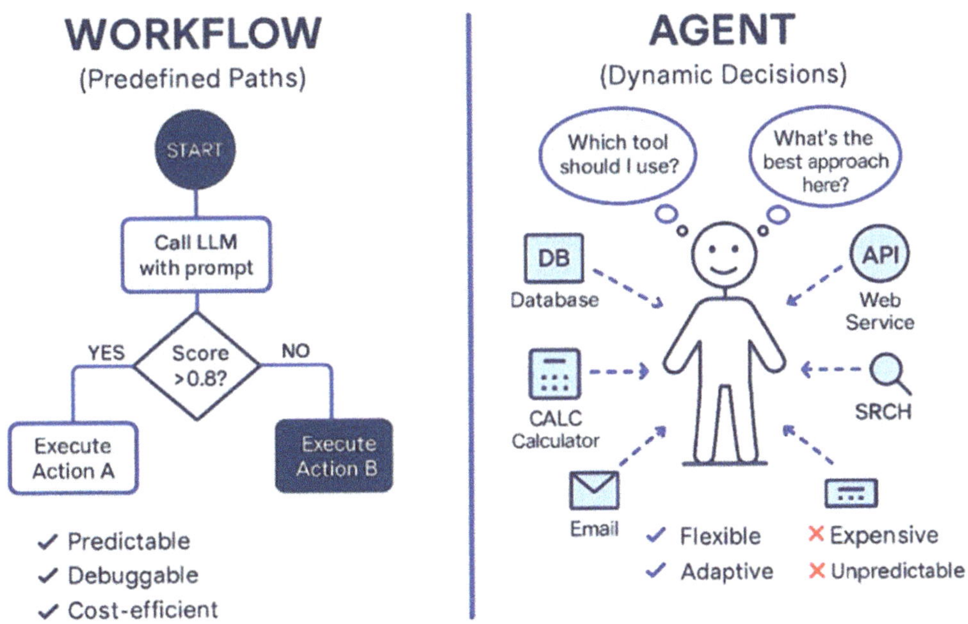

Figure 5.1: Agentic AI workflow model.

Source: *(Neel Shah, 2018)*

It typically entails several related judgments, actions, and validations. This is where the shortcomings of relying solely on cues start to become apparent. For isolated activities, single-prompt usage is effective, but it has trouble with complexity. A more structured approach is required when work calls for accuracy, consistency, and reproducibility throughout multiple phases. Designing AI usage in a way that mimics how actual work is completed is necessary to go beyond simple instructions.

Limitations of Single-Prompt AI Usage

Completing a complicated activity with just one prompt frequently yields unexpected outcomes. The AI attempts to condense several acts into a single response, which raises the possibility of omitting information or misinterpreting intent. This method relies too much on a single command and makes the assumption that AI will do each step correctly on its own.

Some common limitations of single-prompt usage include:

- **Loss of structure in complex tasks**: When multiple actions are requested at once, AI may prioritize some steps while ignoring others. Important details such as data validation or formatting can be skipped unintentionally.

- **Inconsistent outputs across repeated use**: The same prompt may produce different results each time, especially when input data changes. This makes it difficult to rely on AI for recurring tasks like reports or analyses.

- **Difficulty in reviewing and correcting errors**: If the final output is incorrect, it becomes hard to identify which part of the process failed. Users often need to rerun the entire prompt instead of fixing a specific step.

- **Overloading the AI with vague responsibility**: Asking AI to "analyze data and write a report" forces it to make assumptions about analysis methods, priorities, and presentation style, which may not align with organizational needs.

These limitations highlight why single prompts are best suited for simple, one-off tasks rather than real operational work.

Why Real Work Requires Multi-Step Thinking

Tasks in real-world settings are organized logically. Every step relies on the results of the one before it. Creating a survey report, for instance, is a multi-step process. It entails reviewing unstructured data, removing unnecessary entries, spotting trends, summarizing insights, and creating an organized document. Each of these processes has a certain function and calls for a different kind of reasoning. When AI is made to do all of these tasks simultaneously, quality frequently deteriorates. AI can concentrate on one task at a time when work is divided into phases. This enhances accuracy and clarity while reflecting how people operate.

Key reasons why multi-step thinking is essential include:

- **Improved clarity of purpose at each stage**: Each step has a clear objective, such as cleaning data or summarizing themes, which reduces ambiguity.
- **Better control over outputs**: Outputs can be reviewed at intermediate stages instead of only at the end.
- **Easier refinement and correction**: If a mistake occurs, only the affected step needs adjustment rather than the entire workflow.
- **Greater repeatability for recurring tasks**: Structured stages ensure that the same process can be applied consistently across projects.

Multi-step thinking transforms AI from a reactive responder into a reliable process participant.

How Agentic Workflows Solve the Problem

The purpose of agentic workflows is to get over the drawbacks of single prompts. Work is separated into logical stages, each with a specified input and output, rather than depending on a single instruction. Because these phases are linked in a certain order, AI can automatically transition from one task to the next.

AI does not make guesses about what to do next in an agentic workflow. It travels along a predetermined route. This structure guarantees that crucial processes are not omitted and increases dependability. The procedure eventually transforms from a one-time interaction into a reusable solution.

Agentic workflows provide several advantages:

- **Clear separation of responsibilities:** Each stage handles a specific task, such as grouping data or drafting text, reducing confusion.
- **Consistent performance across repetitions**: The same workflow produces similar results even when data changes.
- **Built-in opportunities for review**: Human checkpoints can be added between stages to ensure quality and accuracy.
- **Scalability for larger workloads**: Once tested, the same workflow can handle more data or more frequent execution without redesign.

By connecting stages logically, agentic workflows allow AI to complete complex tasks reliably and repeatedly.

Designing Clear Stages with Purposeful Outputs

The quality of an agentic workflow's stages determines its success. Every step should have a single duty and a well-defined result. This guarantees seamless transitions between steps and avoids overlap.

Effective stage design typically includes:

- **Explicit definition of input data**: AI should know exactly what information it is working with at each stage.
- **Clear description of the task to be performed**: Instructions should focus on one action rather than multiple goals.
- **Well-defined output format**: Outputs should be structured in a way that the next stage can easily use.

This kind of stage design makes AI more predictable and manageable. These workflows can be improved over time without interfering with the process as a whole. Anyone who wishes to employ AI for actual work instead of sporadic help must go beyond single prompts. Organizations can fully realize AI's potential as a reliable partner in intricate, multi-step processes by implementing agentic workflows and organized stages.

5.2 UNDERSTANDING AGENTIC AI IN PRACTICE

Agentic AI represents a practical shift in how synthetic intelligence is implemented to actual work. As opposed to giving AI limitless freedom or treating it as a tool that truly reacts to activates, agentic AI is built across the idea of structured obligation. The intelligence of the machine does no longer come from autonomy on my own, however from clear instructions, defined obstacles, and a carefully designed technique. On this approach, human beings continue to be on top of things even as AI executes tasks constantly and successfully.

At its core, agentic AI is set delegation. Just as a manager assigns work to a worker with clear expectations, an agentic AI workflow assigns obligations to AI with specific policies. The workflow clothier comes to a decision what the AI need to do, the order in which responsibilities have to be completed, and the conditions beneath which the AI need to maintain, pause, or are trying to find review. This clarity transforms AI from an unpredictable assistant into a dependable operational partner.

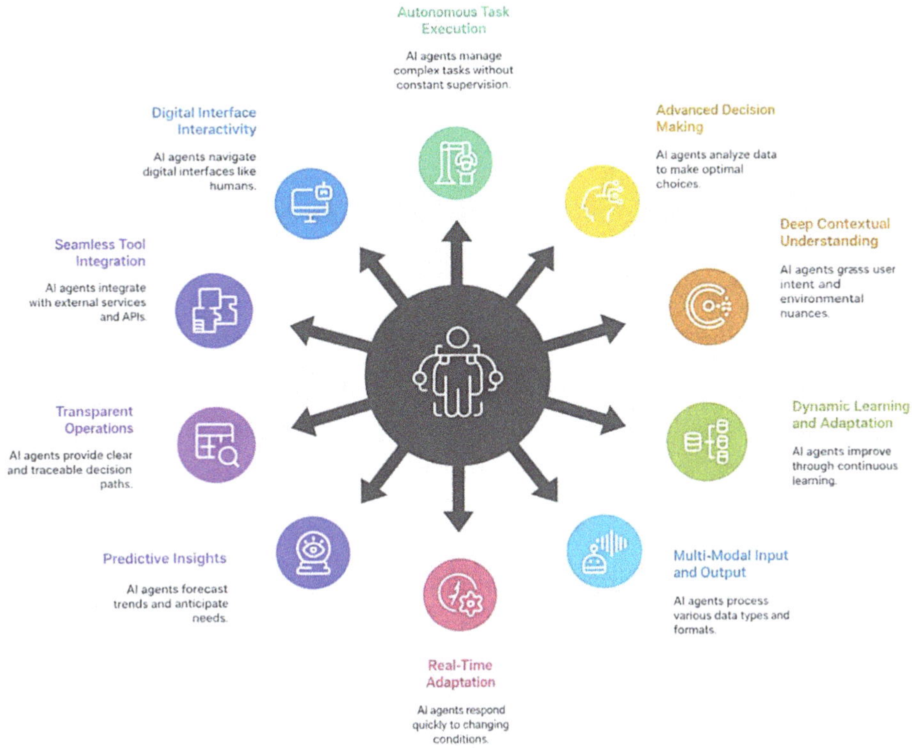

Figure 5.2: Autonomous AI task execution.

Source: *(Aiswarya Madhu, 2020)*

Established obligation rather than unlimited Freedom

A commonplace false impression about superior AI structures is they need to take delivery of complete freedom to function independently. In real organizational environments, this technique often results in inconsistent outputs and lack of trust. Agentic AI takes the other path. It limits freedom intentionally and replaces it with structure. In exercise, agentic AI operates within predefined barriers. Each step in the workflow has a clear cause and anticipated output. AI does no longer determine randomly what to do subsequent. Instead, it follows a chain designed via human beings. This shape guarantees that the AI behaves predictably and aligns with organizational goals. Based obligation additionally improves responsibility.

Due to the fact the workflow is really described, it turns into smooth to trace where selections are made and how outputs are produced. When a blunder occurs, groups can become aware of the specific step that wishes adjustment as opposed to wondering the complete device. This transparency is critical for building lengthy-time period self-assurance in AI-driven processes.

How Agentic AI Operates in actual Workflows

In real-world applications, agentic AI capabilities as a step-following gadget. It receives input, approaches it according to defined rules, and produces output that turns into the input for the following step. At each stage, the AI knows whether to continue robotically or look ahead to human input. For instance, in a survey evaluation workflow, agentic AI may additionally begin with the aid of validating statistics fine. If the records meets predefined requirements, it actions to theme identification. If the facts carry mistakes or missing information, the AI pauses and notifies a human reviewer. This choice-making isn't always based totally on judgment or instinct but on without a doubt described conditions set at some point of workflow design.

Human overview points are an important a part of this system. Agentic AI is designed to understand whilst a project requires context, interpretation, or accountability. At those points, control is intentionally passed again to human beings. This collaboration guarantees that AI enhances paintings rather than replacing critical human judgment. Agentic AI additionally supports consistency throughout repeated obligations. Whilst the identical form of paintings is achieved frequently, consisting of weekly reporting or month-to-month analysis, the AI follows the same system every time. This eliminates variant resulting from fatigue, time pressure, or person interpretation. Consistent execution ends in extra dependable consequences and simpler quality manage.

Why Predictability Makes Agentic AI Effective

In settings where tasks are predictable and repeated, agentic AI functions best. In these activities, the structure doesn't change even if the data does. Report creation, lesson planning, updating documentation, and routine performance analysis are a few examples. AI can apply the same logic repeatedly without confusion thanks to predictability. A workflow can operate with little oversight after it has been tested and improved. Because of this, agentic AI is very helpful for small teams that need to increase output without hiring more people. Additionally, training and maintenance are made easier by repeatable operations. Redesigning procedures for every new work is not necessary for teams.

Rather, they make use of already-existing workflows and only modify them when necessary. This stability guarantees that AI will continue to be a reliable component of daily operations and lessens cognitive stress. The goal of agentic AI is not to replace people in the workforce. It involves creating systems in which human's direct strategy and guarantee quality, while AI manages execution under explicit guidelines. Agentic AI produces dependable outcomes that businesses can rely on and expand upon by fusing organized accountability with predictable operations.

5.3 IDENTIFYING TASKS SUITABLE FOR AUTOMATION

Automation is one of the most attractive promises of agentic AI, but it's also one of the maximum misunderstood. Many companies anticipate that if an undertaking can be defined, it have to be automatic. In truth, now not all responsibilities advantage from automation and applying AI to the incorrect form of paintings regularly creates more issues than it solves. The achievement of agentic AI relies upon in large part on choosing the right duties tasks that observe a clean shape, repeat frequently, and convey comparable sorts of outputs each time.

Figuring out appropriate tasks for automation isn't a technical decision alone. It's far a strategic and realistic workout that requires know-how how paintings without a doubt occurs inner and business enterprise. While performed successfully, automation reduces repetitive attempt and mental fatigue at the same time as retaining human judgment at the center of important choices.

Understanding the character of Repetitive and Predictable work

Agentic AI plays high-quality in environments where work follows a recognizable pattern. Predictable duties are those that repeat frequently with only minor versions in enter. The stairs remain in large part the equal, even though the content might also trade. This predictability lets in AI to follow a defined manner reliably. For instance, record generation in a survey-based totally commercial enterprise typically follows the same collection: gathering data, cleansing responses, identifying themes, summarizing insights, and drafting a report. Although the survey subject matter may alternate, the workflow itself remains strong. In addition, lesson education in academic institutions frequently involves the identical structure week after week, even if subjects fluctuate.

Documentation updates in tech teams additionally observe consistent formats and rules. Those types of duties are mentally demanding but now not conceptually complicated. People spend time repeating the equal steps rather than making use of deep judgment. Agentic AI flourishes in such situations due to the fact it is able to execute predefined steps accurately and consistently, liberating human beings from recurring execution. Predictable paintings also produce outputs that look comparable on every occasion. Reports have sections, lesson plans follow a format, and documentation adheres to standards. When outputs are structured, AI may be skilled or guided to generate them reliably. This consistency is a key sign that a challenge is appropriate for automation.

Spotting duties that require Human Judgment

Even as agentic AI is strong, it has clear barriers. Tasks that depend heavily on emotional intelligence, negotiation, ethics, or long-term strategy have to not be automated. Those responsibilities require context that is going past styles and records. For example, resolving a struggle between crew individuals, negotiating with a consumer, or making strategic commercial enterprise selections entails expertise emotions, intentions, and long-term effects. AI may help by way of imparting records or drafting pointers, but it should not act autonomously in those areas.

Human judgment is important because the cost of errors is excessive and the context is regularly nuanced. Similarly, innovative choice-making that involves originality, vision, or cultural sensitivity is better treated through humans. Whilst AI can generate thoughts or drafts, very last decisions have to remain with those who apprehend the broader implications. Spotting those barriers is vital. Automation has to now not purpose to update human obligation. As an alternative, it should assist human beings by using putting off repetitive work that drains strength and interest.

Defining Clear Task Boundaries before Automation

Before building an agentic workflow, groups must really define wherein a project starts and ends. This step is regularly neglected, but its miles essential for successful automation. Without clear barriers, AI workflows emerge as indistinct, unpredictable, and hard to manipulate. Defining project limitations means specifying what AI is answerable for and what remains underneath human manipulate. As an example, AI can be allowed to analyze survey responses and draft a report, but a human should approve insights earlier than they are shared with clients. In an academic setting, AI may generate assignments; however instructors determine which questions are suitable for their college students. Clear limitations also help manipulate expectations. Groups understand that AI is a tool for execution, no longer an alternative for accountability.

This clarity reduces resistance and builds accept as true with in automation structures. The last intention of agentic AI is not to put off human roles, but to lessen repetitive attempt that consumes time and intellectual power. While automation is applied thoughtfully, it permits people to recognition on interpretation, creativity, and selection-making areas in which human competencies be counted most. Figuring out tasks suitable for automation is therefore a foundational step. It determines whether or not agentic AI turns into a reliable associate or a source of frustration. Via choosing predictable, repeatable duties, respecting human judgment, and defining clear boundaries, groups can free up the actual cost of agentic AI in ordinary work.

5.4 BREAKING WORK INTO CLEAR WORKFLOW STEPS

Giving AI broad, ambiguous instructions won't create a robust agentic AI workflow. It is constructed by meticulously segmenting the work into distinct, doable phases. Every stage should have a specific duty and a well-defined result. This methodical technique turns AI from a generic helper into a dependable digital worker capable of consistently and controllably handling challenging jobs.

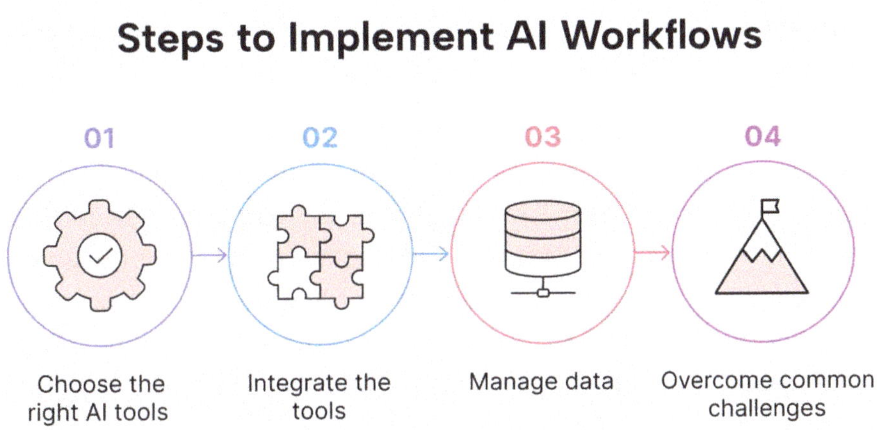

Figure 5.3: Step-based AI workflow.

AI outputs frequently become inconsistent, perplexing, or challenging to verify when work is not adequately broken down. Step-based procedures, on the other hand, make AI behavior more predictable and manageable. This section emphasizes the importance of segmenting work into phases and how doing so enhances agentic AI systems' accuracy, transparency, and trust.

- **Why clear step definition is the foundation of agentic workflows**: In actual-global paintings, responsibilities rarely manifest. They follow a series where one action relies upon on the result of the previous one. Clear step definition mirrors how people naturally work. Whilst each step has a specific cause, AI is aware exactly what it desires to do at that moment. This reduces ambiguity and prevents AI from making assumptions. Clean steps additionally make sure that the workflow remains strong even when information size or content material changes.

- **Single obligation makes AI outputs more dependable: every** step in an agentic workflow must carry out best one characteristic. For instance, validating data ought to no longer additionally involve analysis or summarization. When multiple obligations are blended into one step, mistakes come to be tougher to trace. An unmarried-responsibility step produces centered output, which improves accuracy and makes it easier to pick out wherein things went incorrect if a trouble happens.
- **Nicely-defined outputs enhance consistency across runs:** each step ought to produce a selected type of output, including a wiped clean dataset, a list of issues, or a dependent summary. When outputs are in reality described, AI offers results in a predictable format on every occasion. This consistency is critical for scaling workflows across initiatives, teams, or customers. It also simplifies human review due to the fact reviewers know precisely what to expect from each step.
- **Replacing vague commands with dependent tiers:** Asking AI to "analyze survey information and write a document" combines multiple duties into one guidance. This often ends in mixed-fine results due to the fact AI ought to decide how to method the venture on its personal. With the aid of dividing the equal work into degrees along with facts validation, subject identification, perception extraction, and report drafting, every a part of the process turns into clearer. AI specializes in one objective at a time, generating better-first-rate outputs at every level.
- **Error detection becomes faster and less complicated:** when work is broken into steps, mistakes are simpler to discover. If a final document looks incorrect, groups can trace the issue again to a selected stage, which include subject matter identity or perception extraction. This focused troubleshooting saves time and prevents needless remodel. In preference to rerunning the whole workflow, groups can fix handiest the affected step.
- **Improved transparency for groups and stakeholders:** Step-primarily based workflows make AI interest visible. Groups can virtually see which steps are automatic and wherein human assessment is concerned. This transparency builds self-assurance among group participants who can also otherwise experience unsure about AI-driven procedures. Stakeholders additionally advantage clarity approximately how outcomes are produced, which increase will agree with in AI-supported outputs.

- **Clean separation among AI execution and human judgment:** Breaking paintings into steps allows define in which AI need to act independently and where human judgment is needed. AI can deal with repetitive, records-heavy obligations which include grouping responses or drafting summaries. Humans can evaluation insights, validate accuracy, and make final choices. This separation ensures responsibility whilst nonetheless making the most of automation.
- **Less difficult onboarding and expertise switch:** whilst workflows are certainly documented step by step, new crew participants can apprehend and use AI structures greater fast. They do now not want to guess how obligations are done. Each step explains what AI does and what the predicted outcome is. This reduces dependency on person information and supports lengthy-time period scalability.
- **Better adaptability to exchange:** business requirements evolve, and workflows ought to adapt. Step-based designs make trade easier. If a new requirement arises, teams can regulate or add an unmarried step without remodeling the complete workflow. This flexibility guarantees that agentic AI structures continue to be useful at the same time as techniques and goals shift over time.
- **More potent basis for automation and scaling:** Automation works first-rate while procedures are simply defined. Step-by way of-step workflows offer a sturdy basis for including triggers, conditions, and integrations later. Once steps are stable and dependable, workflows can be scaled to handle larger volumes, greater frequent execution, or extra use instances with confidence. It is not necessary to complicate processes in order to divide work into distinct workflow steps. Making them comprehensible, manageable, and repeatable is the goal. Agentic AI is much more effective in real-world applications, easier to manage, and easier to trust when each step has a defined goal and output.

5.5 DESIGNING INPUTS AND OUTPUTS

Designing inputs and outputs is one of the maximum critical steps in constructing dependable agentic AI workflows. Whilst many human beings attention heavily on activates or gear, the proper balance of an automatic workflow relies upon on how sincerely each step defines what statistics enters the gadget and what result is anticipated at the stop. While inputs and outputs are indistinct or inconsistent, AI behavior turns into unpredictable. Whilst they are absolutely structured, workflows come to be repeatable, correct, and scalable across distinct projects and groups. In agentic workflows, AI does no longer operate in isolation. It actions from one step to some other, carrying facts forward.

If those records are unclear at any factor, mistakes multiply. Considerate design at the enter and output level prevents this hassle and turns AI into a reliable machine as opposed to an experimental device.

Knowledge the function of Inputs in Agentic Workflows

Inputs are the starting point of any AI-pushed mission. They offer context, constraints, and raw fabric for processing. In an agentic workflow, inputs may additionally take many forms, such as uploaded documents, textual content entries, form responses, or established datasets. Regardless of layout, the key requirement is clarity. Whilst inputs are loosely defined, AI must make assumptions. Those assumptions regularly lead to inconsistent or incomplete results. as an example, if a workflow honestly gets "survey information" without specifying layout, scope, or first-rate expectations, AI can also interpret the data differently every time. This modification reduces trust and increases assessment attempt.

Properly-designed inputs consist of clear boundaries. They specify what records is covered, what ought to be unnoticed, and how statistics is prepared. This shape helps AI procedure facts efficaciously and reduces ambiguity. Clean inputs additionally allow people to apprehend what the AI is working with at any stage, which improves transparency and duty. Every other gain of structured inputs is blunders detection. Whilst inputs follow a described layout, it turns into less difficult to pick out lacking or incorrect statistics earlier than the workflow proceeds. This early validation protects downstream steps and ensures that mistakes do not spread for the duration of the process.

Defining Outputs for Consistency and manipulate

Outputs are the tangible consequences of an agentic workflow. They'll seem as summaries, reports, tables, files, or indicators. While the form may additionally range, the purpose remains the equal: to deliver usable outcomes that healthy into real paintings tactics. Poorly described outputs regularly create greater work in preference to saving time. If AI generates consequences in exceptional formats each time, human beings need to spend extra attempt reorganizing or rewriting content. This defeats the purpose of automation. Clean output definitions save you this trouble by using putting expectations in advance.

Effective output layout specifies structure, tone, and stage of detail. When AI knows whether or not it ought to produce a short precis, a detailed file, or a structured desk, it can generate results that require minimal adjustment. This consistency is particularly important whilst workflows are repeated often or shared across teams. Clear outputs additionally support integration. When AI-generated effects are designed to healthy present structures or templates, they can be used at once. This reduces friction and will increase adoption. Over the years, steady outputs construct self-assurance and make AI workflows experience like a natural extension of every day paintings.

Enabling Reusability and Scalability through Structure

One of the best benefits of carefully designed inputs and outputs is reusability. Whilst workflows rely on clean systems as opposed to unique content material, they may be applied to distinct responsibilities without rewriting commands. The equal manner can manage specific datasets, topics, or projects really by using changing the input. Reusability saves time and encourages standardization. Teams can proportion workflows throughout departments or customers without remodeling them for each case. This consistency improves high-quality and decreases gaining knowledge of curves for brand new users. Scalability additionally depends on structure. As workflows expand to handle large volumes of facts or more frequent triggers, clear inputs and outputs save you overall performance degradation.

AI keeps to behave predictably even under improved load because expectations stay consistent. Established layout also simplifies preservation. When workflows need updates, teams can adjust input or output definitions without converting the entire system. This adaptability ensures that agentic AI remains beneficial as organizational wishes evolve. Designing inputs and outputs is not a technical element to be overlooked. Its miles a strategic selection that determines whether or not agentic AI workflows continue to be fragile experiments or grow to be dependable systems. Clean structure transforms AI right into a tool that scales with a bit of luck, adapts without problems, and supplies steady cost throughout real-international programs.

5.6 ADDING TRIGGERS AND CONDITIONS

When agentic AI procedures are independent of manual initiation, they become genuinely effective. When AI understands precisely when to begin, what to check, and how to choose the next course of action, automation truly shines. This is accomplished by carefully utilizing conditions and triggers. When combined, they enable AI to perform like a responsible digital worker, acting only when necessary and adhering to regulations before proceeding. While conditions specify how an AI workflow should continue, triggers specify when the workflow should start. Even a well-designed workflow can become hazardous, unexpected, or ineffective without these two components. This section describes how circumstances and triggers combine to produce scalable, regulated, and dependable agentic processes.

Understanding Triggers in Agentic AI Workflows

Triggers serve as an AI workflow's initial signal. They guarantee that tasks start at the appropriate time and eliminate the need for manual activation. AI workflows should take into account the fact that most jobs in actual work environments are either time-driven or event-driven.

1. **Time-Based Triggers and Their Practical Role**: Time-based triggers activate workflows at predefined intervals. For example, a survey analysis workflow may start every Friday evening, or a weekly lesson planning workflow may run every Sunday night. These triggers are useful for recurring tasks that follow a fixed schedule. They ensure consistency and prevent delays caused by human forgetfulness or workload pressure.
2. **Event-Based Triggers for Real-Time Action**: Event-based triggers activate workflows when a specific action occurs. This could be the upload of new survey data, submission of an online form, or entry of a new lesson topic by a teacher. Event-based triggers allow AI to respond immediately to changes, making workflows more dynamic and responsive.
3. **Reducing Manual Dependency Through Triggers**: When triggers are implemented correctly, teams no longer need to remember to start processes. AI begins work automatically at the right moment. This reduces operational friction and ensures that tasks are completed on time, even during busy periods.

Triggers alone, however, are not enough. They tell AI when to start, but not whether it should continue. This is where conditions become essential.

The Role of Conditions in Decision-Making

Conditions allow AI workflows to make decisions based on data quality, completeness, or predefined rules. They act as checkpoints that determine whether the workflow should proceed, pause, or stop. Without conditions, AI may process flawed data or produce unreliable outputs.

1. **Data Validation Conditions**: one of the most common uses of conditions is checking facts best. For instance, if a survey dataset includes too many incomplete responses, the workflow can stop and notify a human reviewer. This prevents poor-nice data from affecting very last insights.

2. **Good judgment-based progression situations:** conditions can guide workflow development. If certain criteria are met, AI maintains to the following step. If now not, it takes an opportunity course. As an instance, if analysis outcomes meet predefined accuracy thresholds, the workflow may additionally proceed to record era. In any other case, it may request rationalization or extra input.
3. **Hazard control and duty:** conditions shield companies from accidental results. They ensure that AI does not act blindly. Via embedding decision regulations, groups preserve manipulate over touchy obligations which include patron reporting, educational assessment, or software release documentation.

Conditions turn AI from a passive executor into a controlled decision-making system that respects boundaries and quality standards.

Combining Triggers and Conditions for Reliable Automation

When triggers and conditions cooperate, agentic workflows truly shine. Conditions control behavior throughout the workflow, whereas triggers start actions. This combination guarantees that AI works effectively without risk or needless processing.

1. **Preventing Unnecessary AI Processing**: now not each cause has to bring about full execution. For instance, new statistics uploads may arise regularly, but situations can take a look at whether or not enough records exist to justify processing. This prevents wasted computational attempt and reduces noise in outputs.
2. **Creating Human assessment Checkpoints:** Triggers may begin a workflow automatically, but conditions can implement human evaluate at essential degrees. If AI-generated consequences exceed positive thresholds or involve touchy statistics, the workflow can pause and request approval. This stability continues agree with and responsibility.
3. **Making sure Scalability and stability:** As workflows scale across initiatives and groups, triggers and conditions hold consistency. New customers may additionally engage with the device in a different way; however the same guidelines observe universally. This balance makes big-scale automation conceivable and predictable.
4. **Assisting continuous development:** over time, triggers and conditions can be delicate primarily based on experience. Groups can also alter schedules, redefine satisfactory thresholds, or introduce new selection policies. This flexibility permits workflows to conform without redesigning the entire gadget. Adding conditions and triggers is more than just a technical improvement.

It is a calculated move that turns AI workflows into reliable systems compatible with practical operations. When carefully planned, conditions guarantee responsible execution and triggers guarantee prompt action, enabling agentic AI to provide reliable results without continual oversight.

5.7 HUMAN REVIEW AND CONTROL POINTS

Although agentic AI workflows are made to carry out activities on their own, this does not imply that they are free from human accountability. Even the most meticulously designed processes can make mistakes, misinterpret context, or apply regulations too strictly. The stakes increase when clients, students, or end users receive AI outputs. Because of this, human review and control points are crucial parts of any trustworthy agentic AI system and are not optional security measures. While letting AI manage execution at scale, human oversight guarantees accuracy, maintains context, and safeguards trust.

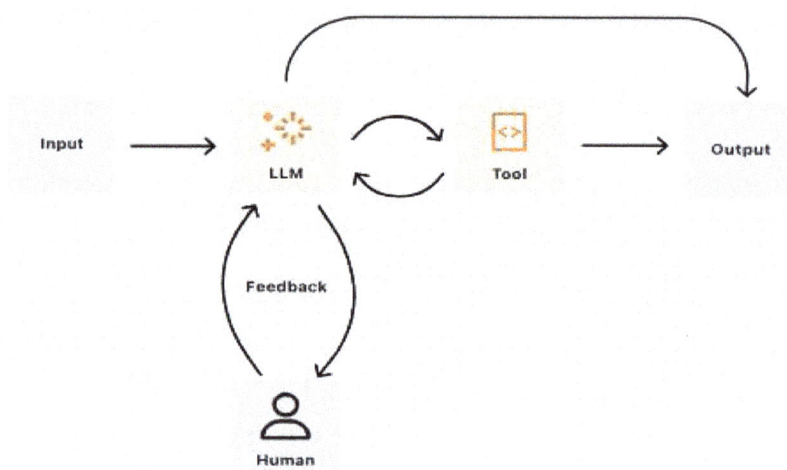

Figure 5.4: Human-in-the-loop control.

Workflows are not slowed down by well-designed control points. Rather, they direct human attention to the most important areas. Organizations can benefit from AI's efficiency without compromising responsibility by combining automated execution with intentional human approval.

Why Human Review Is Essential in Agentic AI Workflows

AI systems operate based on patterns, rules, and instructions. While this makes them fast and consistent, it also means they lack true understanding of intent, nuance, and consequence. Human review fills this gap by applying judgment and responsibility at critical moments.

- **Accuracy verification at decision-sensitive stages**: AI can summarize data, analyze trends, or draft documents, but it may occasionally misinterpret context or miss subtle details. Human reviewers verify facts, check numbers, and confirm that interpretations align with real-world meaning before outputs are finalized.
- **Tone and communication alignment**: while AI generates content for clients, college students, or stakeholders, tone subjects as plenty as accuracy. Human beings ensure that language is suitable, respectful, and aligned with organizational values, something AI can't reliably judge on its own.
- **Contextual judgment and exception dealing with:** actual-international facts frequently consist of exceptions that don't fit general styles. Human reviewers understand when unique coping with is required and can override automatic choices while situations call for flexibility.
- **Moral and reputational protection:** Outputs shared externally convey reputational hazard. Human approval ensures that touchy facts are treated responsibly and that messages do no longer create misunderstanding, bias, or unintended damage.

Human review does not replace AI efficiency; it enhances it by ensuring that automation delivers dependable results.

Designing Effective Control Points without Slowing Work

The effectiveness of human oversight depends on where and how control points are placed. Too many review steps create friction, while too few increase risk. The goal is balance: AI executes routine work, and humans intervene only at meaningful checkpoints.

- **Strategic placement of review stages**: control factors should be positioned before outputs are shared externally or used for choices. Internal processing steps can continue to be absolutely automated, whilst very last outputs pass thru human approval.
- **Clear obligation for approval:** every manage factor ought to have a described owner. When obligation is unclear, evaluations become inconsistent. Assigning clear accountability guarantees that outputs are checked efficiently and decisively.
- **Described standards for assessment decisions:** Human reviewers should know exactly what to test. Standards including accuracy, completeness, tone, and compliance lessen subjective judgment and speed up approvals.

- **Escalation regulations for complex cases:** some outputs may require additional attention. Clear escalation paths make sure that complex or touchy cases receive suitable evaluate without blockading routine work.
- **Remarks loops for non-stop development:** Human corrections have to feed back into the workflow. Whilst reviewers continuously regulate certain outputs, activates and rules may be delicate, reducing destiny evaluation attempt.

Control points function as quality gates rather than barriers when they are intelligently built. They maintain speed while safeguarding results. Agentic AI is transformed from a dangerous automation experiment into a reliable working system through human review and control points. Organizations make sure that AI stays a tool for execution rather than a substitute for accountability by retaining people in control of final approval and judgment.

5.8 TESTING AND REFINING AGENTIC WORKFLOWS

The automation path doesn't end with creating an agentic AI workflow. When exposed to real-world data, even well-designed procedures might exhibit unpredictable behavior. Variations in input quality, unforeseen edge cases, or ambiguous instructions frequently don't become apparent until after actual use has started. Because of this, testing and improving agentic workflows is a crucial stage in determining whether AI becomes a dependable system or a source of frequent corrections. While ongoing improvement guarantees long-term stability and trust, careful testing on small samples enables teams to learn safely. Agentic workflows are not intended to be flawless from the outset. As they are used, they get better. Businesses that view AI workflows as dynamic systems outperform those that demand instant perfection.

Testing Agentic Workflows on Small Samples

Testing is the process of observing how an agentic workflow behaves under controlled conditions. Instead of deploying automation across all data or projects, teams should begin with limited samples that represent real usage without carrying high risk.

1. **Validating Instructions and Workflow Logic**: Small-pattern testing famous whether or not instructions are clear and logically ordered. If AI produces inconsistent or irrelevant outputs, it frequently indicates uncertain activates or lacking steps. Early trying out makes it simpler to accurate these problems earlier than they have an effect on large workflows.

2. **Identifying missing conditions and Safeguards:** real statistics often behaves in a different way than anticipated. Trying out enables discover conditions wherein workflows proceed once they need to pause or stop. Lacking conditions emerge as visible, allowing teams to add safeguards which includes best assessments or evaluate factors.
3. **Comparing Output fine and Relevance:** testing allows teams to decide whether AI outputs meet realistic standards. Despite the fact that technically correct, outputs can be too typical or misaligned with enterprise or educational desires. Reviewing small samples makes it less difficult to refine tone, depth, and structure.
4. **Gazing mistakes styles and part instances:** positive inputs always purpose problems. Small-sample trying out allows perceive those patterns early. Groups can then design responses for part cases instead of reacting to errors after complete deployment.
5. **Constructing team self-belief through safe Experimentation:** checking out on restrained facts reduces worry and resistance. Group individuals see how AI behaves without risking important errors. This self-belief is critical for lengthy-term adoption.

Small-sample testing is not about speed. It is about understanding behavior. The insights gained at this stage guide all future improvements.

Refining Workflows for Long-Term Reliability

Refinement begins once testing reveals how the workflow behaves in real conditions. Unlike traditional software, agentic AI improves through incremental adjustments rather than complete rewrites. Refinement focuses on improving clarity, consistency, and usefulness over time.

1. **Improving Prompts Based on Real Feedback**: activates have to evolve based on located outputs. When AI responses miss context or produce inconsistent consequences, prompts can be adjusted to include clearer instructions or constraints. Those small adjustments often cause considerable first-class upgrades.
2. **Adjusting Workflow Steps for higher glide:** testing might also monitor unnecessary steps or missing transitions. Refinement permits groups to simplify workflows or upload intermediate steps wherein wished. Clear waft reduces confusion and improves execution velocity.

3. **Enhancing Output structure and format:** Outputs ought to come to be more established through the years. Refinement may also contain standardizing headings, summaries, or codecs so that consequences require minimum human enhancing. Established outputs growth performance and usefulness.
4. **Lowering Human review attempt step by step:** As workflows grow to be more reliable, teams can modify review factors. Early ranges may require near oversight, even as mature workflows allow lighter evaluation. This slow shift will increase automation without sacrificing first-class.
5. **Monitoring Consistency throughout Repeated Runs:** Repetition famous stability. Refinement specializes in making sure that comparable inputs produce similar outputs over the years. Consistency builds trust and lets in workflows to scale expectantly.
6. **Scaling best After balance Is executed:** Refinement have to precede expansion. Once outputs are regular and predictable, workflows can take care of large datasets or greater common triggers. Scaling without refinement increases threat.

Testing and refining agentic workflows is a continuous discipline, not a one-time task. By starting small, learning from real behavior, and making steady improvements, organizations transform AI from an experimental tool into a dependable system that supports real work reliably.

5.9 DEPLOYING AGENTIC AI SAFELY

Deploying agentic AI workflows in live surroundings marks a critical transition from experimentation to real operational use. At this stage, AI structures are no longer confined to controlled assessments or restricted datasets. They begin interacting with real records, actual users, and real results.

Due to this, secure deployment isn't always clearly a technical step, however an organizational duty. A considerate deployment method guarantees that AI workflows supply fee consistently whilst ultimate aligned with enterprise or institutional objectives.Safe deployment begins with the know-how that AI systems are dynamic.

Their performance can exchange over the years as facts patterns shift, consumer conduct evolves, or workflows scale. Corporations that treat deployment as a one-time movement often face sudden problems later. In assessment, those who view deployment as the begin of an ongoing control technique are higher organized to maintain reliability and agree with.

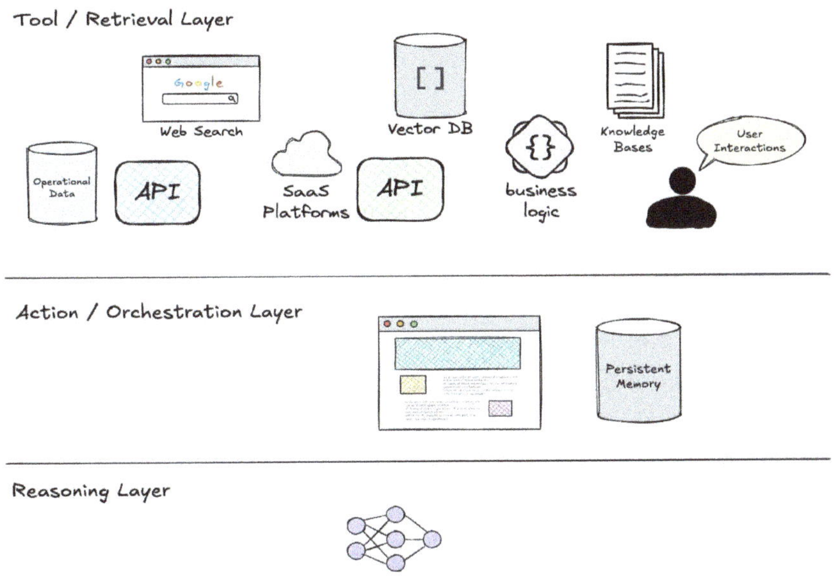

Figure 5.5: **Agentic AI system architecture.**

Monitoring and Governance in stay Environments

Once an agentic workflow is going stay, continuous monitoring becomes important. Monitoring lets in teams to understand how AI behaves underneath real conditions and whether or not outputs stay accurate and beneficial. This doesn't require complex dashboards or advanced analytics. Simple performance indicators which include turnaround time, errors frequency, and the quantity of human corrections provide valuable insights into machine fitness. Monitoring errors is mainly vital in the course of early deployment. Errors may additionally get up from surprising records codecs, area cases, or uncertain commands. When those issues are identified fast, groups can modify activates, refine situations, or introduce additional evaluate factors. Early detection prevents small issues from escalating into large failures that harm accepts as true with inside the gadget.

Alignment with organizational dreams is some other key component of safe deployment. AI workflows have to be evaluated no longer handiest on technical performance, however additionally on whether they guide supposed consequences. For example, a survey evaluation workflow ought to improve insight fine and transport velocity, while an academic workflow must support gaining knowledge of goals rather than actually growing automation. Regular opinions help make sure that AI keeps to serve its motive as opposed to drifting in the direction of performance at the fee of exceptional. Clear documentation performs a critical position in governance. Documentation explains how workflows perform, what records they use, and in which human oversight is needed. This transparency permits groups to manage AI structures hopefully and reduces dependence on an unmarried expert.

When obligations are sincerely described, troubles can be addressed speedy without confusion or put off. Deploying agentic AI accurately also entails preparing human beings. Teams need to apprehend how workflows function, what their function is in review and approval, and how to respond when something goes wrong. Schooling does not need to be complicated; however it ought to be steady. Whilst users experience knowledgeable and supported, they may be more likely to consider and undertake AI structures fully. Through the years, adequately deployed agentic AI will become a stable part of every day operations. It supports work quietly in the history; dealing with ordinary execution even as human's awareness on decision-making and improvement. This balance turns AI from a quick-time period test into a protracted-term productiveness associate that grows alongside the agency.

A. SHORT QUESTIONS

1. What is meant by agentic AI?
2. How is agentic AI different from single-prompt AI usage?
3. Why are agentic AI workflows important for automation?
4. What types of tasks are suitable for agentic AI workflows?
5. Explain the role of workflow steps in agentic AI systems.
6. What is the importance of defining inputs and outputs in AI workflows?
7. Why triggers are used in agentic AI workflows?
8. Explain the concept of human-in-the-loop in agentic AI.
9. Why is testing important before deploying agentic AI workflows?
10. How does agentic AI improve productivity in organizations?

B. LONG QUESTIONS

1. Explain the concept of agentic AI workflows and how they differ from traditional AI usage.
2. Describe the steps involved in designing an effective agentic AI workflow.
3. Discuss the importance of human review and control points in agentic AI systems.
4. Explain how triggers and conditions improve the reliability of agentic AI workflows.
5. Analyze the benefits and challenges of deploying agentic AI in real-world organizations.

C. MULTIPLE CHOICE QUESTIONS (MCQS)

1. Agentic AI primarily focuses on:

   a) Answering isolated questions
   b) Performing multi-step tasks autonomously
   c) Replacing human decision-making
   d) Providing theoretical knowledge

2. Which feature distinguishes agentic AI from basic AI tools?

   a) Single-prompt responses
   b) Random outputs
   c) Structured workflows
   d) Manual execution

3. Tasks best suited for agentic AI are those that are:

   a) Emotional and subjective
   b) Creative and unpredictable
   c) Repetitive and structured
   d) Ethical in nature

4. Human-in-the-loop means:

   a) Humans are removed from workflows
   b) AI works without supervision
   c) Humans review and approve AI outputs
   d) AI replaces managers

5. Why is breaking work into steps important in agentic AI?

   a) To increase complexity
   b) To reduce clarity
   c) To improve reliability and control
   d) To avoid automation

6. Inputs and outputs in AI workflows should be:

   a) Unclear and flexible
   b) Randomly defined
   c) Clearly structured
   d) Ignored

7. Triggers in agentic AI workflows are used to:

   a) Stop AI completely
   b) Decide when the workflow starts
   c) Remove human review
   d) Generate random actions

8. Testing agentic AI workflows helps to:

   a) Eliminate human involvement
   b) Identify errors and improve accuracy
   c) Increase automation risks
   d) Delay implementation

9. Deploying agentic AI safely requires:

a) No monitoring
b) Complete automation
c) Human oversight and controls
d) Ignoring outputs

10. Agentic AI improves productivity by:

a) Increasing workload
b) Reducing structured work
c) Automating repeatable tasks
d) Eliminating accountability

CHAPTER 6

BLUEPRINTS FOR REAL-WORLD IMPACT

6.1 WHY BLUEPRINTS MATTER

Many corporations undertake AI with high expectancies, yet fail to acquire lasting results. In maximum cases, the hassle is not the great of the AI gear getting used. Modern AI structures are effective, on hand, and able to managing complex duties. The real motive for failure is the absence of clear workflows. Teams frequently use AI randomly, making use of it to remoted obligations without knowledge how the ones responsibilities join within a larger technique. This unstructured utilization creates confusion, inconsistent consequences, and subsequently frustration.

Blueprints deal with this specific problem. They provide a clean shape that shows how AI fits into actual paintings. In place of treating AI as a group of disconnected functions, blueprints flip it into a coordinated system. when groups comply with a blueprint, they recognize no longer handiest what AI does, but also whilst it need to act, how it ought to technique records, and where human oversight is needed.

Blueprints as the inspiration of clean AI Workflows

A blueprint defines the whole journey of labor from beginning to cease. It explains wherein AI enters the process, what inputs it gets, how it transforms the ones inputs, and what outputs it produces. Just as importantly, it highlights where people review effects and make final decisions. This clarity gets rid of uncertainty and helps groups work with confidence. Whilst workflows are unclear, extraordinary group members may use AI in distinct methods. One individual may additionally depend heavily on automation, even as every other avoids it entirely. This inconsistency reduces performance and makes effects unpredictable. A blueprint creates shared information. Absolutely everyone is aware of how the workflow operates and what role AI performs at every stage.

Blueprints additionally lessen resistance to AI adoption. When people recognize the technique, they're much less possibly to experience that AI is replacing them or behaving unpredictably. As an alternative, they see AI as a based assistant that supports their paintings. This transparency builds believe and encourages wider adoption across groups. Any other important gain of blueprints is repeatability. Once a workflow is sincerely described, it may be reused across projects without beginning from scratch. The same blueprint may be applied to one of a kind datasets, customers, or obligations with minimum adjustment. This saves time and ensures regular pleasant.

Blueprints also make scaling less difficult. As groups develop or handle larger volumes of work, dependent workflows prevent chaos. AI keeps to operate inside described obstacles, while call for will increase. Groups can refine and enhance blueprints over the years; however the center shape remains strong. In essence, blueprints flip AI from an experimental tool into a dependable machine. They offer direction, reduce confusion, and make sure that AI supplies cost continuously. Without blueprints, AI usage remains scattered and fragile. With them, AI turns into an included part of everyday work, supporting humans rather than overwhelming them.

6.2 SURVEY BUSINESS AI BLUEPRINT

Survey-driven agencies paintings at the intersection of numbers and narratives. Alongside established records such as ratings and more than one-desire solutions, they ought to also interpret open-ended feedback filled with evaluations, feelings, and context. Coping with both varieties of records simultaneously is tough, in particular while response volumes develop. The Survey enterprise AI Blueprint is designed to cope with this genuine venture via changing raw responses into clean, patron-prepared insights through a managed and efficient workflow. This blueprint isn't about adding complexity. Its miles approximately developing a dependable system wherein AI handles repetitive processing while human beings hold duty for interpretation and final transport. Whilst applied effectively, it enables survey companies to scale operations without compromising best or increasing group size.

From raw Responses to established know-how

The blueprint begins on the factor of facts collection. Survey responses arrive from more than one channel and often comprise inconsistencies which include duplicates, incomplete solutions, and variations in language. Manually making ready this statistics consumes extensive time and often delays evaluation. AI streamlines this early stage via reviewing the dataset as quickly as its miles accumulated. AI cleans the information with the aid of getting rid of duplicate entries, flagging incomplete responses, and standardizing textual content wherein essential. This creates a reliable dataset that is ready for deeper analysis.

As soon as the information is prepared, AI actions to the interpretation stage, wherein it reads open-ended responses and identifies habitual subject matters. Feedback that explicit similar ideas are grouped together, permitting patterns to emerge certainly. This thematic grouping transforms overwhelming volumes of feedback into potential insight categories. Analysts not want to study every response in my opinion. As an alternative, they evaluate grouped subject matters that constitute the collective voice of respondents. This stage brings readability and pace, making it feasible to understand client sentiment at scale without losing vital nuances.

Turning Insights into client-equipped Deliverables

After patterns are diagnosed, the blueprint actions from analysis to conversation. AI drafts an insight record that translates findings into based narratives. Those drafts usually consist of summaries of key subject matters, discovered traits, and initial suggestions based on the statistics. The motive is not to replace human understanding, but to provide a robust starting point. Human reviewers then step in to validate the findings. They test whether the insights align with commercial enterprise context, refine language to match purchaser expectations, and ensure that hints are realistic and actionable. This evaluation degree protects nice and maintains responsibility at the same time as nevertheless making the most of AI-pushed efficiency.

Once finalized, the record is ready for shipping. Due to the fact lots of the foundation has been automatic, turnaround time is substantially decreased. Clients obtain insights faster, and groups enjoy much less fatigue from repetitive evaluation paintings. This blueprint lets in survey agencies to develop confidently. Larger datasets and additional customers no longer translate into heavier workloads. As an alternative, AI absorbs the growth in quantity, while human information ensures insight pleasant stays high. By means of combining structured automation with considerate assessment, the Survey enterprise AI Blueprint creates a sustainable version for handing over value at scale.

6.3 EDUCATION INSTITUTION AI BLUEPRINT

Academic institutions function on routines that repeat week after week and month after month. Lesson making plans, task advent, assessment, reporting, and verbal exchange observe predictable cycles aligned with academic calendars. This predictability makes education one of the maximum suitable domains for dependent AI assist. An education group AI blueprint does now not aim to update teachers or directors. As a substitute, it provides a clear framework wherein AI supports education, analysis, and communique at the same time as educators keep manipulate over teaching and pupil interaction. The cause of this blueprint is to reduce the invisible workload that surrounds teaching. A lot of an educator's time is spent outside the classroom making ready materials, checking work, compiling reports, and drafting messages. By way of organizing those sports into a coherent AI-supported workflow, institutions can improve performance without compromising instructional exceptional or human judgment.

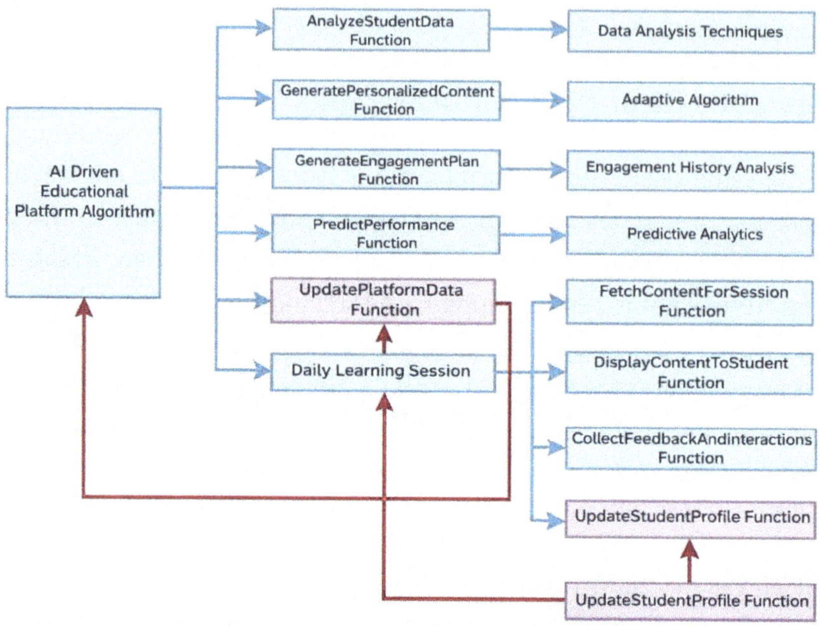

Figure 6.1: Education AI blueprint.

Structuring educational paintings round cyclical techniques

Instructional work is inherently cyclical. Each week begins with making plans, keeps with preparation and assessment, and ends with overview and reporting. The training AI blueprint aligns directly with this rhythm, making sure that AI support suits evidently into existing practices in place of disrupting them. The workflow starts with lesson making plans. When curriculum info which includes problem, grade stage, subject matter, and mastering effects are supplied, AI generates dependent lesson outlines. These outlines encompass targets, advised activities, and pacing steerage. Instructors evaluate these drafts, alter them primarily based on school room realities, and finalize the plan. This technique gets rid of the need to begin from scratch each week whilst preserving expert autonomy.

Once lesson plans are accredited, the workflow moves to mission and worksheet introduction. AI generates academic substances that align with the defined goals. This ensures coherence among what is taught and what is assessed. Teachers select, refine, or adapt these substances to suit their college students' desires, saving time even as retaining educational purpose. After education and evaluation, AI assists with grading assist and performance analysis. It helps become aware of not unusual errors, patterns of misunderstanding, and regions in which students may also need additional aid. Instructors continue to be answerable for final evaluation, however AI affords readability that could in any other case require hours of guide evaluation.

To keep the workflow focused and manageable, the education blueprint emphasizes three core operational areas:

1. **Weekly instructional preparation and material generation**: This includes lesson outlines, classroom activities, assignments, and practice exercises generated in alignment with curriculum goals and teaching schedules.
2. **Assessment review and performance insight generation**: AI supports the analysis of test results and assignments, helping educators understand trends, learning gaps, and progress patterns across classes or individual students.
3. **Administrative and parent communication support**: AI drafts progress summaries, internal reports, and parent-facing communication, which teachers and administrators personalize before sharing.

These three areas form the backbone of the education AI blueprint, covering most recurring academic tasks without interfering with classroom teaching.

From Assessment to Communication and Continuous Support

The second one half of the schooling institution blueprint focuses on what occurs after coaching and evaluation. This degree is often underestimated, yet it consumes a big portion of educators' time. AI plays a treasured role by way of organizing data and making ready clean drafts that guide informed decision-making and verbal exchange. After checks are completed, AI analyzes consequences to provide overall performance summaries. Those summaries highlight strengths, weaknesses, and trends at each the person and class level. Instructors use these facts to modify future lesson plans, layout remedial activities, or offer centered help. The blueprint ensures that evaluation information will become actionable insight instead of static information. Communication is the very last level of the workflow. Colleges and faculties are required to speak often with dad and mom and inner stakeholders.

Writing newsletters, development updates, and administrative reviews is repetitive but touchy paintings. AI assists via drafting clear and dependent messages primarily based on existing statistics. Instructors and administrators evaluation those drafts to make certain accuracy, tone, and context earlier than sharing them externally. This dependent method ensures consistency across communique whilst decreasing the time educators spend on repetitive writing. Greater importantly, it allows educators to attention on meaningful engagement with college students and dad and mom instead of administrative formatting.

The education group AI blueprint is designed to be bendy. Colleges can implement it step by step, beginning with lesson making plans or evaluation and expanding over the years. Due to the fact the workflow mirrors existing instructional cycles, adoption feels natural in place of compelled. Through integrating AI into predictable academic procedures, this blueprint ensures that educators spend less time getting ready and processing facts and greater time teaching, mentoring, and supporting students. The end result isn't always just accelerated efficiency, but extra sustainable and human-targeted instructional surroundings.

6.4 SMALL TECH TEAM AI BLUEPRINT

The viability of small tech teams depends on their ability to work quickly, clearly, and consistently. Inefficiencies swiftly escalate into delays and quality problems when there is a small team size and several tasks assigned to the same people. The Small Tech Team AI Blueprint is intended to include AI in a regulated and useful way throughout the whole development lifecycle.

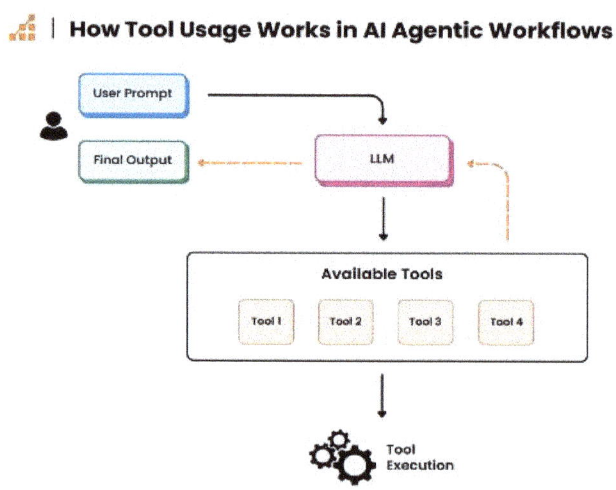

Figure 6.2: Tech team AI blueprint.

Source: *(Guilherme Assemany, 2025)*

This plan integrates AI into routine development tasks rather than treating it as a stand-alone tool, enabling teams to increase production without adding complexity or losing control. The goal of this design is to assist developers, product managers, and testers by minimizing repetitive work while maintaining the importance of human judgment in decision-making.

AI Integration across the Development Lifecycle

The development lifecycle in a small tech team typically moves through predictable stages, starting from requirement intake and ending with release and communication. AI fits naturally into each of these stages when applied thoughtfully.

1. **Requirement Intake and Clarification**: The workflow starts when characteristic requests or worm reviews arrive from users, stakeholders, or inner discussions. These inputs are often unstructured and scattered throughout emails, tickets, or chat messages. AI summarizes these raw inputs into clear requirement descriptions, highlighting middle wishes, constraints, and anticipated results. This structured interpretation reduces ambiguity and ensures that the team begins improvement with a shared knowledge.
2. **Assignment Structuring and making plans guide:** once requirements are clarified, AI converts them into dependent development responsibilities. These responsibilities encompass context, scope, and reputation expectations, making them simpler to estimate and prioritize. This level improves making plans accuracy and reduces again-and-forth verbal exchange, permitting teams to transport quicker with confidence.
3. **Coding and Documentation help:** at some stage in improvement, AI supports builders by helping with boilerplate code technology and suggesting patterns that align with the assignment to hand. On the identical time, AI drafts technical documentation primarily based on code remarks and development notes. This ensures that documentation evolves alongside the code instead of becoming an afterthought.

Testing, Release, and Human Control Points

Beyond development, the blueprint extends AI support into testing and release activities while preserving essential human oversight.

1. **Testing Support and Bug Handling**: AI assists testers and developers via suggesting check instances primarily based on feature behavior and capability edge

scenarios. It also summarizes computer virus reviews in clear language, making them simpler to apprehend and reproduce. This improves test insurance and reduces the time spent interpreting poorly written reviews.

2. **Launch Notes and Deployment Summaries:** At the release degree, AI generates draft release notes and deployment summaries by means of studying finished obligations and changes. Those drafts observe a regular structure, saving time and ensuring clean verbal exchange with stakeholders and customers. Human reviewers validate technical accuracy and modify messaging as needed.
3. **Human evaluate and exceptional guarantee:** during the lifecycle, human evaluation remains critical. Important stages which includes requirement approval, very last testing, and release verbal exchange encompass mandatory evaluate points. Those checkpoints ensure alignment with product dreams, save you errors, and keep duty.
4. **Scalability without added Complexity:** due to the fact the blueprint is predicated on established workflows as opposed to ad-hoc automation; it scales smoothly. As assignment extent increases, the equal AI-supported methods can deal with extra work without overwhelming the group. This scalability permits small tech groups to develop output while retaining excellent and consistency.

The Small Tech Team AI Blueprint demonstrates how AI can be embedded across the development lifecycle in a balanced and practical way. By supporting requirements, development, testing, and release activities, AI becomes a reliable partner that enhances productivity while keeping humans firmly in control.

6.5 END-TO-END WORKFLOW VISIBILITY

One of the maximum valuable advantages of the use of dependent AI blueprints is the visibility they devise throughout a business enterprise's workflows. While paintings procedures are definitely defined and smooth to understand, groups advantage a shared view of how obligations flow from start to complete. This readability reduces confusion, minimizes duplicated attempt, and strengthens duty at every level of execution. In place of counting on assumptions or informal knowledge, absolutely everyone concerned can see precisely in which work begins, the way it progresses, and in which it ends.

In lots of agencies, especially small groups, workflows evolve informally over time. Responsibilities are dealt with based totally on experience as opposed to documented approaches. Whilst this could work in the early degrees, it often leads to inefficiencies as teams grow or workloads growth. AI blueprints deliver shape to those workflows through making every step seen and intentional. This visibility will become the inspiration for both operational efficiency and believe in computerized systems.

How Visibility Improves manage, Optimization, and consider

While workflows are seen, groups can effortlessly discover wherein time and effort are being spent. Bottlenecks that had been formerly hidden turn out to be clear. For example, delays in approval, repeated guide exams, or unnecessary handovers stand out while the whole procedure is mapped visually. Once those problems are visible, teams can make informed selections about optimization. They are able to determine which steps benefit maximum from automation and which require stronger human oversight. Visibility additionally improves responsibility. When roles and responsibilities are truely linked to workflow levels, possession becomes specific. Crew members realize who is answerable for each step, reducing confusion and preventing responsibilities from being overlooked.

This clarity encourages proactive problem-solving and decreases the chance of errors due to miscommunication. Any other crucial benefit of visible workflows is the balance it creates between automation and human manage. AI is powerful; however it must no longer operate in isolation. Clean workflow visibility permits groups to determine wherein AI have to take the lead and where human judgment need to remain important. This balance guarantees that automation complements productivity without compromising satisfactory or moral obligation. Believe in AI systems grows certainly whilst workflows are obvious. Whilst human beings recognize how choices are made and why positive actions arise, they're more likely to just accept and depend upon automated outputs.

Visibility removes the perception of AI as a "black container" and replaces it with confidence grounded in information. Groups now not question whether AI is appearing randomly; they see the common sense behind every step. In the long time, workflow visibility helps continuous development. As groups benefit revel in, they can refine techniques, modify automation ranges, and improve effects with out disrupting operations. Clear workflows make it simpler to adapt to alternate, scale operations, and keep consistency across initiatives. By making paintings visible, AI blueprints flip automation into a collaborative and honest device that supports both human beings and overall performance.

6.6 REUSABLE TEMPLATES AND PROMPT SAMPLES

AI blueprints supply actual cost only while they are supported through shape. Without structure, AI outputs range in layout, tone, and depth, forcing humans to spend greater time correcting outcomes. Reusable templates and spark off samples clear up this problem by using developing consistency. They turn AI from an experimental tool into a reliable machine that produces predictable, usable consequences throughout distinct initiatives and teams. Templates and spark off samples act as the muse of scalable AI workflows. They define how data enters the gadget, how it's far processed, and how consequences are delivered. While designed carefully, they lessen trial-and-error, accelerate adoption, and make certain exceptional stays constant while usage grows.

The function of Reusable Templates in AI Workflows

Reusable templates offer a hard and fast structure for AI inputs and outputs. They ensure that each mission follows the identical sample, no matter who initiates it or while it runs. This standardization is particularly critical in environments where a couple of people use AI for comparable responsibilities.

Templates help in several practical ways:

- **Standardizing report structures**: while AI generates reports the usage of a predefined shape, each record consists of the equal sections in the same order. This makes reviews easier to read, evaluation, and evaluate across customers or time durations.
- **Growing steady lesson plan formats:** In academic workflows, templates make sure that lesson plans usually include goals, sports, exams, and timelines. Instructors can recognition on content nice as opposed to formatting.
- **Defining clear mission description layouts:** For tech groups, templates ensure that every mission description includes context, scope, and anticipated consequences. This reduces confusion and improves improvement performance.
- **Producing uniform feedback summaries:** comments templates help AI generate responses which can be balanced, clear, and professional. This consistency is especially beneficial when comments are shared with students, customers, or group members. Reusable templates also simplify collaboration.

When everyone uses the same structure, reviewing and approving AI-generated outputs becomes faster. Over time, templates evolve into organizational standards that reflect best practices rather than individual preferences.

Using Prompt Samples to Guide AI Behavior

While templates define structure, prompt samples define behavior. A prompt sample is a tested instruction that guides how AI should think, analyze, and respond to a task. Instead of writing new prompts every time, teams reuse prompt samples that are already proven to work well.

Prompt samples reduce uncertainty and improve output quality in several ways:

- **Reducing trial-and-error during task execution**: AI is given consistent instructions when a prompt sample is reused. This expedites workflow execution and does away with the need for repetitive experimentation.
- **Preserving clarity and tone:** Prompt samples aid in regulating tone, level of detail, and linguistic style. When AI outputs are disseminated externally, this is very crucial.
- **Ensuring task-specific accuracy:** Different reasoning techniques are needed for different tasks. Prompt samples guarantee that AI consistently concentrates on the appropriate components of the work.
- **Assisting with new user onboarding:** New team members don't require in-depth AI knowledge to utilize the prompt samples that are already in place. This promotes adoption and reduces the learning curve.

Prompt samples should be improved over time in light of actual usage. Teams may identify areas for improvement or reoccurring mistakes. Accuracy and relevancy can be improved without completely altering the workflow by gradually tweaking the prompt wording. A solid foundation for AI-powered work is created by combining prompt examples with reusable templates. Together, templates and timely examples provide AI the structure and guidance it needs to produce reliable outcomes at scale. AI workflows become quicker, more dependable, and more in line with actual organizational needs as teams improve these components.

6.7 MEASURING PRODUCTIVITY AND TIME SAVINGS

Imposing AI workflows is simplest step one closer to transformation. The actual value of AI becomes visible whilst corporations measure how lots paintings have certainly advanced. productiveness and time savings aren't summary thoughts; they may be realistic signs that display whether or not AI is making day by day operations faster, greater dependable, and extra consistent. Without dimension, AI stays a test. With measurement, it becomes a strategic enterprise asset. Many businesses adopt AI with excessive expectancies but fail to music effects systematically. As an end result, it becomes hard to justify continued use or expansion. Measuring productivity and time financial savings gives readability. It suggests in which AI provides price and wherein workflows need refinement.

Know-how productivity profits After AI Implementation

Productivity improvement isn't always only approximately doing more work in less time. It also includes lowering rework, enhancing consistency, and minimizing mental attempt. AI regularly adjustments how paintings are executed rather than in reality dashing it up. As an instance, a challenge that when required several guide steps may additionally now follow a streamlined workflow where AI handles guidance and human's cognizance on assessment. One of the most seen productivity signs is turnaround time. While AI assists with records analysis, content generation, or reporting, tasks that when took days can regularly be completed in hours. Quicker turnaround improves responsiveness and allows groups to deal with a better quantity of labor without growing team of workers.

Every other essential factor of productivity is mistakes reduction. Guide paintings, in particular repetitive paintings, are liable to errors caused by fatigue or oversight. AI applies the same policies always, decreasing variability in outputs. Fewer mistakes suggest less time spent correcting errors and more time spent on meaningful analysis and selection-making. Consistency is likewise a key productiveness indicator. Whilst similar tasks produce comparable outputs, workflows turn out to be predictable and less complicated to manage. AI-pushed strategies help this consistency through following based commands every time. This reliability simplifies planning and improves team self-assurance within the effects.

Tracking Time Savings and Quality Improvements

Time financial savings emerge as significant whilst they are tracked in relation to unique workflows. Groups have to compare how long a venture took before AI implementation and how long it takes after automation. Even small time financial savings in step with assignment can lead to sizable gains when repeated across weeks or months. Exceptional improvements are similarly important. AI does now not simply reduce time; it often improves the readability and shape of outputs. Reports come to be more uniform, documentation stays updated, and evaluation follows constant standards. Those upgrades beautify professional credibility and decrease the need for big revisions. Measuring great does now not require complicated systems.

Simple observations, together with fewer revisions asked through clients or decreased rationalization requests from stakeholders, imply improvement. Through the years, those qualitative indicators translate into tangible business benefits inclusive of better purchaser pleasure and stronger internal confidence. Time financial savings and fine improvements together provide a balanced view of AI impact. Whilst each improves simultaneously, it turns into clean that AI is contributing real price instead of merely moving paintings round.

Turning measurement into non-stop Optimization

Dimension ought to no longer be handled as a one-time interest. Ongoing monitoring permits agencies to perceive traits and refine workflows constantly. While metrics display declining overall performance or extended assessment attempt, it indicators the want for set off modifications or clearer commands. Over the years, measurement statistics publications smarter choices approximately scaling AI.

Workflows that display strong time financial savings and outputs can be multiplied properly. Much less powerful workflows may be redesigned or limited. This facts-pushed technique reduces hazard and guarantees sustainable increase.

6.8 CUSTOMIZING BLUEPRINTS FOR YOUR TEAM

Every enterprise operates inside its very own specific surroundings, formed by means of its people, methods, desires, and constraints. Because of this, no unmarried AI workflow or blueprint can in shape each crew flawlessly. While blueprints provide a treasured start line, their real energy lies in flexibility. They're intended to be tailored thoughtfully in place of followed blindly. Customization lets in teams to align AI workflows with the way work is already accomplished, ensuring that technology supports day by day operations instead of interrupting them. Whilst teams try and practice a blueprint exactly as its miles, they frequently face resistance or confusion.

Present tactics may not match the assumptions built right into a universal workflow. Approval structures, timelines, information formats, and satisfactory expectancies can differ appreciably from one company to every other. By means of adjusting steps and overview factors, groups make sure that AI suits evidently into their mounted routines. This reduces friction and makes adoption feel like a development in place of a compelled alternate. Customization additionally lets in groups to govern the level of automation. No longer all organizations are secure giving AI the identical degree of obligation. Some teams may choose AI to help with coaching and evaluation whilst preserving very last selections completely human-driven.

Others may be prepared to automate whole workflows with minimal oversight. Both methods are legitimate. The key's choosing an automation degree that fits the team's self-belief, enjoy, and danger tolerance. Slow automation builds believe and allows people to study from real use instead of assumptions. Every other essential factor of customization is aligning AI workflows with team skills. Groups with confined technical enjoy can also require less complicated workflows and clearer overview checkpoints. Extra experienced groups can be cozy managing complicated, multi-step automation. Adjusting workflows based totally on talent degree prevents frustration and encourages constant use. Whilst human beings sense successful in place of overwhelmed, adoption turns into sustainable. Customization also facilitates guard existing strengths.

Many corporations have already got green methods that paintings well. AI needs to enhance these strengths, no longer replace them unnecessarily. With the aid of integrating AI into acquainted workflows, groups maintain institutional understanding at the same time as improving efficiency. This method guarantees continuity and avoids the disruption that frequently accompanies surprising technological exchange. Starting small is in particular critical when customizing AI blueprints. Implementing one tailored workflow permits groups to have a look at how AI performs in actual conditions. Remarks from day by day use highlights what works and what desires improvement.

Through the years, workflows can be subtle, multiplied, or mixed with other strategies. This sluggish approach ends in stronger structures that evolve with the agency rather than turning into outdated. Lengthy-term adoption relies upon on comfort and self-assurance. When teams sense that AI workflows reflect their needs and values, they are much more likely to use them continually. Customization transforms AI from an outside tool into an incorporated a part of normal paintings. By means of adapting blueprints thoughtfully and expanding regularly, companies create AI structures which can be realistic, depended on, and able to handing over lasting fee.

6.9 IMLIEMENTING BLUEPRINTS STEP BY STEP

It is not necessary to deploy everything at once in order to successfully implement AI designs. Because they accelerate the process and demand quick transformation, many firms fail at using AI. Sustainable implementation actually occurs gradually.

Teams may gain confidence, comprehend how AI fits into their actual workplace, and address problems early on before expanding further using a methodical strategy. Blueprints are neither one-time setups nor static documents. These are useful systems that change as teams gain knowledge from actual use. Stability, acceptance, and long-term success are ensured by approaching implementation as a phased process.

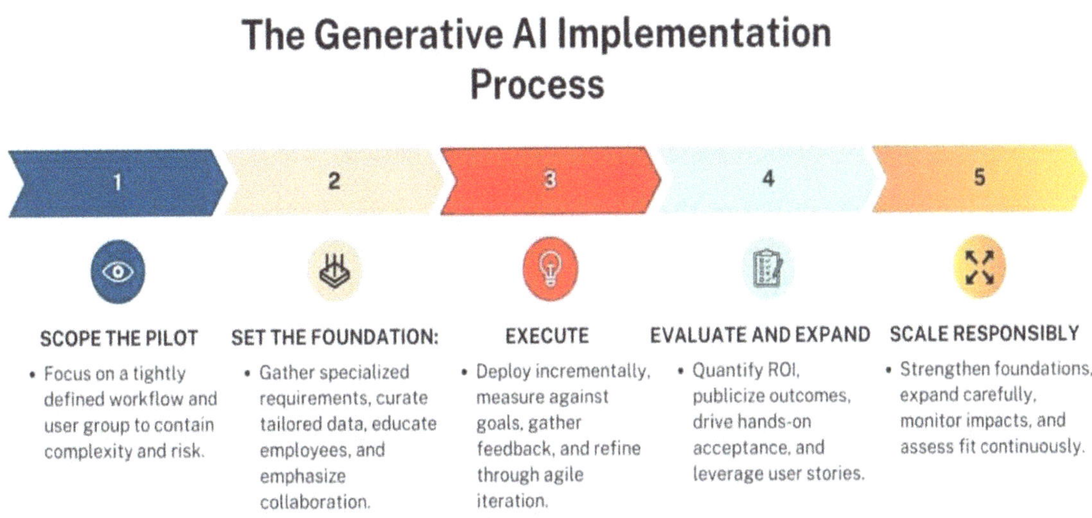

Figure 6.3: End-to-end AI implementation.

Source: *(Sunil Ramlochan, 2021)*

Phased Implementation for Sustainable Adoption

A phased approach helps organizations move from experimentation to reliable daily usage without overwhelming teams or disrupting existing processes. Each phase has a clear purpose and builds upon the previous one.

1. **Selecting a Single Blueprint to Start With**: step one is selecting one blueprint that addresses a repetitive and properly-understood mission. This will be a survey analysis workflow, a weekly lesson planning process, or a documentation workflow for a tech group. Beginning with a single blueprint continues the scope practicable and permits teams to awareness on gaining knowledge of as opposed to juggling more than one structure at once.
2. **Testing the Blueprint in actual situations:** as soon as a blueprint is selected, it must be examined the use of actual records and real work situations. This phase is vital as it famous gaps that won't be seen at some stage in planning. Teams can take a look at how AI handles real inputs, in which outputs want refinement, and how much human overview is required. Checking out in actual conditions builds realistic understanding and stops unrealistic expectancies.
3. **Amassing feedback from customers:** remarks from group members the use of the blueprint day by day is vital. Customers regularly notice small problems consisting

of uncertain outputs, missing context, or formatting troubles. This remarks helps refine prompts, templates, and overview checkpoints. Related to customers early additionally will increase attractiveness, as they experience a part of the implementation method instead of forced into a new device.

4. **Refining and Stabilizing the Workflow:** After initial testing, the blueprint has to be adjusted based totally on comments and observations. Refinement may additionally consist of enhancing commands, including validation steps, or defining clearer human assessment points. This degree specializes in making the workflow dependable and predictable in order that users can accept as true with the consequences always.

5. **Constructing self-assurance via Repetition:** self-belief in AI structures grows with repeated a hit use. While teams see that the blueprint produces consistent outcomes through the years, resistance clearly decreases. This stage is about habit formation. AI turns into a part of recurring work in preference to a unique device used from time to time.

6. **Expanding to additional Workflows:** as soon as the primary blueprint is strong, groups can introduce extra workflows the usage of the same standards. Every new blueprint benefits from lessons found out earlier, making implementation quicker and smoother. This gradual expansion prevents overload and ensures first-class is maintained as AI usage grows.

7. **Encouraging Organizational trust in AI structures:** consider is built when AI behaves predictably and remains below human control. Clear documentation, obvious tactics, and defined duties help teams understand how choices are made. Through the years, AI shifts from being viewed as an experiment to being diagnosed as a dependable help machine.

8. **Treating Blueprints as residing structures:** Blueprints have to never be considered very last. As statistics changes, desires evolve, and teams grow, workflows should adapt. Regular evaluations and small improvements hold blueprints applicable and effective. This continuous evolution guarantees that AI structures improve with use in preference to turning into old.

By implementing AI blueprints step by step, organizations reduce risk, improve adoption, and create systems that deliver long-term value. This disciplined approach allows AI to integrate naturally into daily work while maintaining human oversight and organizational confidence.

A. SHORT QUESTIONS

1. What is meant by an AI blueprint?
2. Why are blueprints important for successful AI implementation?
3. How do AI blueprints improve workflow clarity?
4. What is the role of standardization in AI blueprints?
5. How do blueprints support repeatable AI workflows?
6. Explain the survey business AI blueprint in brief.
7. How does an education institution AI blueprint help teachers and administrators?
8. What is the purpose of a small tech team AI blueprint?
9. How do reusable templates strengthen AI blueprints?
10. Why is step-by-step implementation important when using AI blueprints?

B. LONG QUESTIONS

1. Explain the concept of AI blueprints and their role in achieving real-world impact.
2. Describe the AI blueprint for survey-driven businesses with suitable examples.
3. Discuss how AI blueprints can be applied in educational institutions.
4. Explain the importance of AI blueprints for small tech teams.
5. Analyze how AI blueprints help organizations scale AI usage effectively.

C. MULTIPLE CHOICE QUESTIONS (MCQS)

1. An AI blueprint mainly represents:

   a) A theoretical AI model　**b)** A random automation process
   c) A structured end-to-end workflow　**d)** A coding algorithm

2. The primary purpose of AI blueprints is to:

   a) Increase complexity　**b)** Provide clear workflow structure
   c) Replace human roles　**d)** Delay implementation

3. Which organization benefits most from survey business AI blueprints?

   a) Manufacturing companies　**b)** Survey-driven service providers
   c) Retail stores　**d)** Logistics firms

4. AI blueprints are especially useful because they are:

   a) One-time solutions　**b)** Difficult to understand
   c) Reusable and adaptable　**d)** Unstructured

5. In education, AI blueprints mainly support:

a) Infrastructure development
b) Teaching and administrative workflows
c) Student discipline systems
d) Campus security

6. Small tech team AI blueprints help primarily by:

a) Increasing staff size
b) Replacing developers
c) Organizing development workflows
d) Eliminating planning

7. Templates used in AI blueprints help in:

a) Creating confusion
b) Reducing consistency
c) Standardizing outputs
d) Ignoring quality

8. Step-by-step implementation of AI blueprints ensures:

a) Faster confusion
b) Higher risk
c) Controlled and stable adoption
d) Immediate perfection

9. Which stage is common to most AI blueprints?

a) Random execution
b) Clear input and output definition
c) Removing human review
d) Avoiding automation

10. The main advantage of using AI blueprints is:

a) Increased manual work
b) Clear, scalable AI implementation
c) Reduced productivity
d) Higher operational risk

CHAPTER 7

OPTIMIZATION, TROUBLESHOOTING, AND SCALING

7.1 COMMON ISSUES IN AI WORKFLOWS

Synthetic intelligence is increasingly more used to simplify work, automate strategies, and enhance productiveness. But, when AI workflows do not deliver predicted consequences, groups regularly count on that the generation itself is flawed. In fact, maximum AI-related troubles aren't because of technical screw ups. They normally emerge from uncertain instructions, poor-satisfactory input facts, or unrealistic expectations about what AI can do without steering. Understanding those troubles is crucial for the use of AI efficaciously and enhancing workflows through the years as opposed to leaving behind them in advance. AI systems are incredibly depending on how they're informed and what facts they get hold of. Whilst workflows are designed without clarity or structure, even the most advanced AI tools can produce vulnerable or confusing outputs.

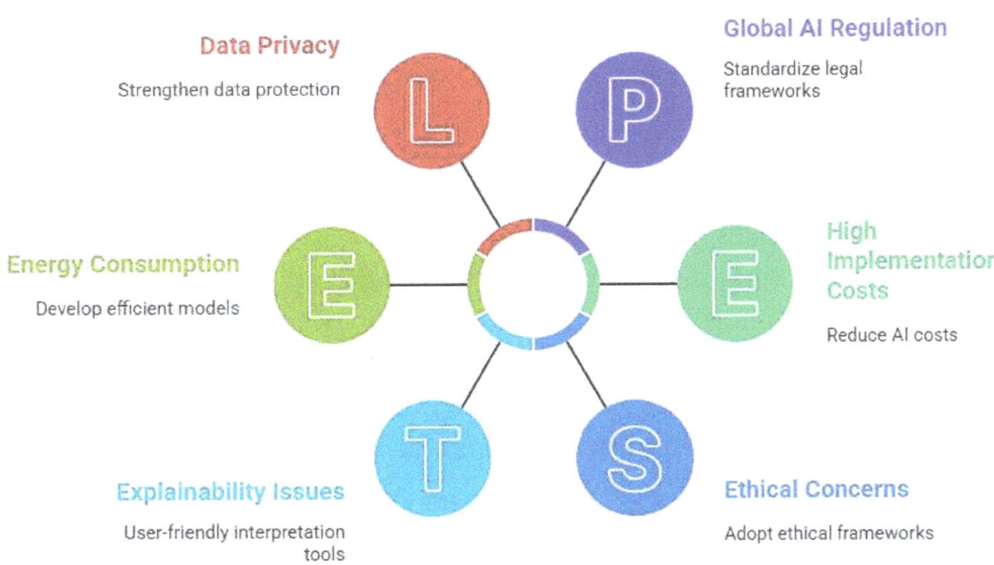

Figure 7.1: Common AI workflow issues.

Source: *(Pavan Vadapalli, 2025)*

Those challenges are part of the learning curve of AI adoption and need to be handled as opportunities for refinement in preference to signs and symptoms of failure.

Uncertain commands and susceptible Workflow layout

One of the maximum commonplace sources of problems in AI workflows is unclear or incomplete commands. AI does not understand rationale in the identical manner human beings do. It is predicated entirely on the steering it is given. Whilst responsibilities are vaguely defined or more than one expectation is blended right into an unmarried guidance, the output regularly will become inconsistent or unfocused. As an example, if AI is requested to "examine feedback and create a report" without specifying the shape, depth, or motive of the document, the consequences may also range on every occasion the task is administered.

In one example, the output can be overly unique, even as in every other it could be too brief or usual. This inconsistency is not a failure of AI intelligence but a reflection of doubtful workflow design. Every other difficulty arises whilst workflows aren't damaged into logical steps. Complicated tasks typically require multiple degrees together with facts cleaning, analysis, interpretation, and presentation. While all of those steps are merged into one training, AI has no clear precedence and might miss critical information. Structured workflows with in reality described steps appreciably reduce errors and enhance reliability.

Statistics nice and Context Misinterpretation

Negative data first-class is some other main motive AI workflows conflict. AI systems paintings nice when the input information is clean, applicable, and nicely-organized. While data consists of duplicates, missing values, beside the point content material, or inconsistent formats, AI may also generate summaries that are incomplete or misleading. Context misinterpretation regularly happens while AI is given uncooked records without enough background records. For example, survey responses, assist tickets, or student data may also incorporate abbreviations, casual language, or domain-unique phrases. Without proper context, AI may additionally misunderstand the means of positive inputs and produce wrong interpretations.

This difficulty becomes extra visible in text-heavy workflows along with summarization and perception era. AI may cognizance on floor-level patterns while missing diffused however vital information. Human oversight is critical at this degree to ensure that context is preserved and that outputs align with actual-world which means. Improving records great and adding contextual steering significantly enhances AI performance. Simple steps including cleansing inputs, defining terminology, and clarifying the reason of analysis can appreciably reduce misinterpretation.

Unrealistic Expectations and Overreliance on AI

Many groups expect AI to supply perfect consequences from the very beginning. This expectation leads to frustration when outputs require revision or human overview. AI isn't a completed product that works perfectly without adjustment. It is a machine that improves via new release and remarks. Overreliance on AI without assessment is some other not unusual mistake. When groups trust AI outputs blindly, mistakes go omitted and self-belief within the machine eventually declines. This creates a cycle in which AI is both overused and completely rejected. An extra sustainable approach is to deal with AI as a collaborative tool. AI handles repetitive processing and sample reputation, at the same time as human beings offer judgment, context, and validation.

When evaluate checkpoints are built into workflows, groups remain in control and errors are stuck early. Information that AI workflows improve progressively facilitates groups continue to be patient and focused on long-time period advantages. Small refinements in prompts, inputs, and evaluate procedures frequently because enormous upgrades in output best. Recognizing not unusual issues which includes doubtful commands, poor information quality, and unrealistic expectations allows corporations to reply calmly and strategically. Instead of viewing problems as failures, groups can treat them as alerts to regulate workflow design and usage practices. This mindset turns AI adoption into a non-stop improvement procedure in place of a one-time test.

7.2 IMPROVING ACCURACY AND CONSISTENCY

Accuracy and consistency are the 2 most vital elements that decide whether or not AI workflows achieve actual-global environments. While AI outputs are unreliable or range broadly from assignment to mission, consider inside the gadget speedy breaks down. Enhancing those factors does now not require advanced technical skills or complicated structures. It relies upon in large part on how without a doubt AI is guided and how dependent the overall workflow is. Nicely-designed AI systems do now not enhance randomly. They improve thru clarity, field, and gradual refinement. While companies apprehend this precept, AI shifts from being unpredictable to turning into a reliable a part of daily work.

Clean guidance as the muse of Accuracy

Accuracy starts offevolved with how instructions are given to AI. Indistinct or loosely defined instructions nearly always result in vague results. While AI is asked to "analyze records" or "summarize feedback" without additional context, it need to wager what topics most. Those guesses may additionally on occasion be beneficial, but they are rarely unique enough for professional use.

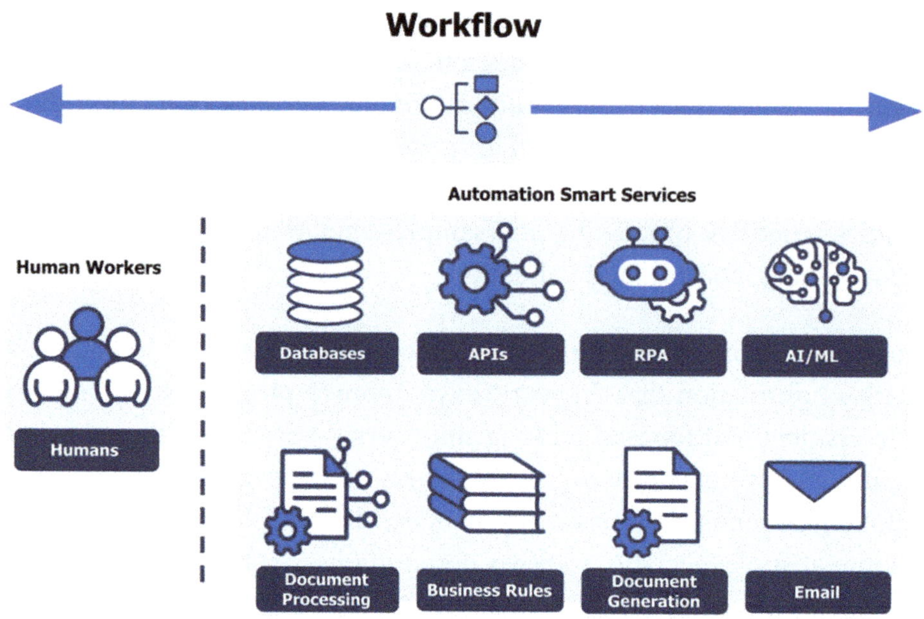

Figure 7.2: Improving AI accuracy.

Source: *(Dan O'Keefe, 2018)*

Clear steerage eliminates ambiguity. Whilst AI is informed exactly what to look for, what to disregard, and the way to structure its output, the consequences come to be a ways more correct. Accuracy improves similarly while inputs are properly organized. Clean information, clear context, and described expectancies permit AI to focus on the mission instead of deciphering motive. Every other vital aspect is proscribing scope. AI plays high-quality while tasks are narrowly described.

Asking it to finish one clear obligation at a time produces better consequences than asking it to deal with multiple targets in an unmarried step. Overloaded instructions often reduce accuracy due to the fact priorities are doubtful. Accuracy additionally improves through overview and adjustment. Whilst groups observe AI outputs and pick out small errors or misunderstandings, they could refine commands for that reason. These refinements acquire over the years, leading to great improvements in exceptional without requiring essential modifications.

Standardization as the Key to Consistency

While accuracy makes a speciality of correctness, consistency makes a speciality of reliability. Consistent AI outputs permit teams to consider results and scale workflows with a bit of luck. Inconsistent outputs, despite the fact that individually correct, create confusion and boom overview time. Consistency improves whilst AI receives inputs within the same format on every occasion. Fixed templates, described systems, and widespread records layouts reduce version. When AI recognizes acquainted patterns, it responds in predictable ways. This predictability makes outputs simpler to check, examine, and reuse. Defined formats also help keep tone and shape.

Whether or not producing reviews, lesson plans, or documentation, consistency guarantees that outputs comply with the identical logical waft. That is mainly essential in organizations in which a couple of human beings depend on AI-generated content. Consistent outputs reduce the need for large editing and alignment. Some other crucial detail is process repetition. Whilst AI workflows are repeated often the use of the identical steps, outcomes stabilize certainly. Every repetition reinforces what works and famous what wishes adjustment. Over time, variability decreases and reliability increases. Consistency is likewise supported with the aid of human oversight. When reviewers observe the same evaluation standards for AI outputs, remarks will become extra powerful. Instead of reacting emotionally to occasional mistakes, teams focus on systematic improvement.

The strength of Small Refinements over time

One of the most omitted aspects of AI optimization is the effect of small, regular refinements. Many corporations assume dramatic enhancements from massive modifications, but real development normally comes from incremental adjustments. A minor change in practise wording can improve readability. A small template adjustment can reduce confusion. A short review checklist can seize routine errors. Personally, these modifications may additionally seem insignificant. Collectively, they rework output satisfactory over time. Everyday refinement also prevents stagnation. As records, requirements, and organizational goals evolve, AI workflows must evolve as properly.

Small updates keep structures aligned with actual desires and save you slow decline in relevance or accuracy. Importantly, this method reduces threat. As opposed to redesigning workflows completely, groups improve them adequately and predictably. Self-assurance grows as AI turns into greater reliable with every new release. Improving accuracy and consistency isn't always approximately perfection. It's far approximately manipulated, readability, and dedication to continuous development. While AI is guided clearly, standardized efficaciously, and refined often, it will become a strong and depended on accomplice in ordinary work in preference to an unpredictable device.

7.3 PROMPT REFINEMENT TECHNIQUES

The basis for AI's comprehension and execution of a task is prompts. They serve as precise guidelines that direct the system toward the desired result. AI frequently produces inconsistent, generic, or erroneous results when suggestions are unclear, lacking, or poorly designed. Conversely, well-crafted prompts produce dependable, consistent, and superior results. Prompt refining is a continuing process that directly affects productivity and trust in AI systems for businesses that use AI in everyday activities.

Many teams erroneously believe that AI malfunctions indicate the tool's inherent unreliability. In actuality, the framing of instructions is frequently the problem. The goal of prompt refining is to enhance human-AI communication so that expectations are understood. Gradually improving prompts based on actual usage yields much better outcomes and long-term stability than starting from scratch every time something goes wrong.

The Core Elements of an Effective Prompt

An effective prompt gives AI enough clarity to perform the task correctly without confusion. It sets boundaries, defines expectations, and reduces guesswork. The following descriptive numbered points explain the most important elements that make prompts stronger and more dependable.

1. **Clear Definition of the Task**: the primary responsibility of a set off is to without a doubt provide an explanation for what the AI is predicted to do. Ambiguous instructions frequently bring about outputs that miss the real goal. When the task is defined precisely, AI cans attention on execution rather than interpretation. As an example, asking AI to "analyze survey responses and generate insights" is some distance more effective than without a doubt announcing "examine these records," as it clarifies the cause of the analysis.
2. **Unique Output expectancies:** AI plays better whilst it is aware of what the final output ought to seem like. Specifying whether or not the result should be a paragraph, a structured record, a precis, or a formatted table improves consistency. While output expectations are simply said, teams spend less time editing and reformatting outcomes, which will increase universal performance.

3. **Described Scope and Constraints:** activates must manual AI on what to consist of and what to keep away from. Citing constraints consisting of phrase limits, tone, audience type, or recognition regions prevents overly broad or irrelevant responses. Constraints act as boundaries that keep AI aligned with real-global necessities and decrease useless facts.

4. **Context for better know-how:** supplying history statistics facilitates AI produce greater applicable outputs. Context such as enterprise type, goal users, or enterprise desires permits AI to tailor its response appropriately. Without context, AI may also produce regular results that require extensive human correction.

5. **Instruction for Consistency throughout Repeated responsibilities:** whilst activates are used regularly, consistency turns into critical. Using standardized language and structure in prompts guarantees that comparable obligations produce comparable outcomes on every occasion. This is specifically crucial for workflows like record technology, lesson making plans, or documentation, where uniformity subjects.

6. **Incremental Refinement based totally on errors:** set off refinement ought to be pushed through statement in preference to assumptions. While outputs incorporate mistakes or gaps, small adjustments to the spark off are regularly enough. Converting one coaching at a time enables groups apprehend what improves results and what does no longer. This slow method prevents instability and saves time in comparison to rewriting activates totally.

7. **Trying out prompts with real statistics:** activates must always be tested the use of real or practical information. Trying out exhibits weaknesses that might not be seen in concept. By means of gazing how AI responds to actual inputs, groups can refine commands to handle aspect instances and enhance reliability before full deployment.

8. **Documenting confirmed activates:** as soon as a prompt continuously produces right effects, it should be documented and reused. Spark off documentation allows groups scale AI utilization, onboard new customers, and preserve exceptional across departments. This practice turns person mastering into organizational expertise.

Prompt refinement is a skill that improves with practice and patience. Teams that invest time in refining prompts gradually build stable AI workflows that deliver dependable results. Instead of treating prompts as casual instructions, successful organizations treat them as structured tools that evolve alongside their processes.

7.4 HANDLING ERRORS AND EXCEPTIONS

No gadget, whether or not human-driven or automated, is absolutely unfastened from errors. This fact applies equally to AI-powered workflows. Even as AI can significantly reduce manual attempt and enhance velocity, it isn't resistant to errors. The actual electricity of a dependable AI machine lies not in warding off errors absolutely, however in how correctly the ones errors are detected, managed, and corrected. Well-designed blunders managing ensure that AI stays a trusted partner rather than an unstable dependency.

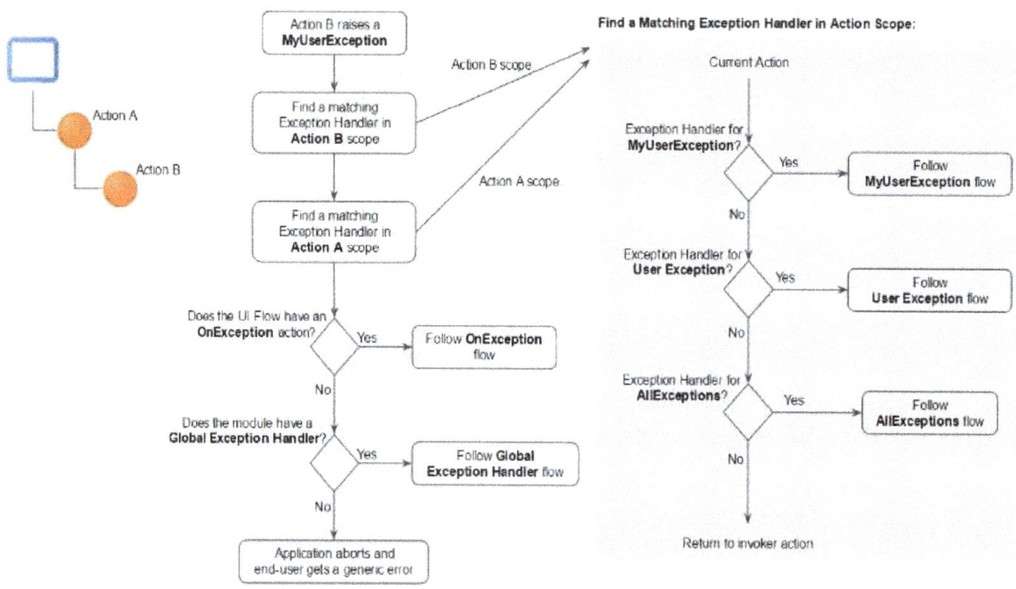

Figure 7.3: AI error handling process.

In realistic environments which include businesses, faculties, or tech groups, errors left unchecked can unfold quick. A small mistake in data evaluation can have an effect on a whole report, a grading error can misrepresent scholar overall performance, and a technical oversight can lead to faulty releases. Dealing with mistakes thoughtfully is therefore essential for long-term AI adoption.

Designing AI Workflows That stumble on errors Early

The first step in handling errors is accepting that they may arise. As soon as this mindset is followed, workflows may be designed to trap problems early as opposed to permitting them to drift through the machine unnoticed. That is wherein checkpoints become crucial.

Checkpoints are intentional pauses in an AI workflow in which outputs are reviewed earlier than transferring to the next level. As an instance, after AI generates a summary or analyzes records, the workflow need to no longer at once proceed to final reporting. rather, it must pause and permit a human reviewer to verify whether the output makes feel, whether the tone is suitable, and whether key information are accurate. These review moments prevent small inaccuracies from turning into larger issues. Early detection also improves performance. Solving blunders at the beginning of a workflow takes some distance less time than correcting it after more than one step have already been finished. By means of constructing evaluate tiers into the system, groups benefit manipulate over AI outputs without slowing down average productivity.

Managing Exceptions and Maintaining Human Control

Exceptions arise when AI encounters situations outside its normal operating patterns. This could include incomplete statistics, contradictory inputs, or uncommon eventualities that have been not expected at some point of workflow design. In such cases, AI ought to no longer try and force a solution. Instead, it must be designed to apprehend uncertainty and request human enter. Pausing a workflow when something seems wrong is not a weak spot; it's far a signal of a mature gadget. Human intervention on the proper second ensures that context, judgment, and enjoy are carried out wherein AI on my own may additionally fall quick. This collaboration between AI and human beings strengthens responsibility and decreases chance.

Over the years, patterns in errors and exceptions provide precious mastering possibilities. Groups can refine activates, adjust policies, and enhance records great primarily based on real-international experience. This non-stop improvement cycle makes workflows greater dependable and adaptable. Most importantly, it builds consider among customers. When human beings recognize that AI systems are monitored and managed, they're greater inclined to rely on them for critical responsibilities. Errors dealing with are ultimately approximately responsibility. AI may assist with execution, but human beings remain liable for effects. By way of designing workflows that detect mistakes early, control exceptions gracefully, and maintain human oversight, groups ensure that AI complements reliability in preference to undermining it.

7.5 MONITORING AI PERFORMANCE

As agencies start to rely on AI workflows in their each day operations, tracking performance turns into a critical obligation. Imposing AI is not a one-time activity. Its effectiveness depends on how properly it continues to perform over the years underneath real working conditions. Without monitoring, groups may also assume that AI is operating efficiently whilst small inaccuracies quietly lessen exceptional and agree with. Tracking guarantees that AI remains dependable, beneficial, and aligned with organizational desires.

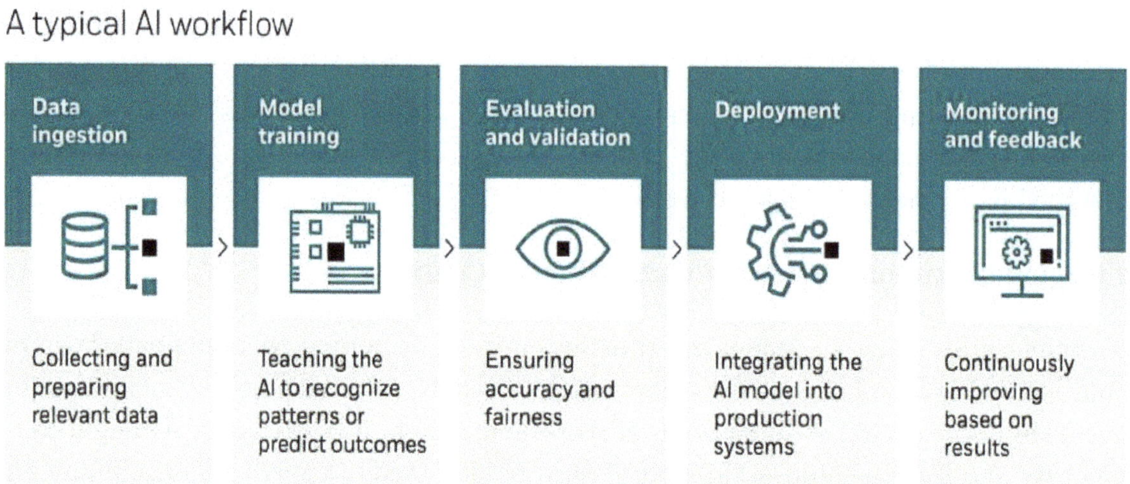

Figure 7.4: AI performance monitoring.

AI performance monitoring does no longer require advanced analytics systems or complex dashboards. In reality, easy and steady remark often can provide higher consequences than overly technical size structures. The cause of monitoring isn't to control AI excessively, however to understand how it behaves in real workflows and the way its outputs affect humans and techniques. While groups frequently observe AI performance, they benefit readability approximately what is working well and what wishes improvement. This recognition allows corporations circulate from experimental use to strong, lengthy-time period adoption.

Why Regular Monitoring Matters

AI structures examine patterns from records and commands; however actual-international environments are continuously changing. Facts codecs evolve, enterprise priorities shift, and person expectancies develop. Without everyday tracking, AI workflows may additionally slowly drift away from their authentic cause. Outputs may additionally turn out to be less accurate, less applicable, or less regular over the years. Monitoring lets in groups to detect such changes early. For example, if an AI-generated report requires greater human corrections than before, it indicators that prompts, statistics excellent, or workflow logic can also need adjustment. Early detection prevents small issues from turning into large operational problems. Any other vital cause for tracking is agreed with. Humans are extra inclined to work with AI after they experience confident about its reliability. When teams recognize that AI outputs are regularly reviewed and stepped forward, they are more likely to depend on them for vital responsibilities. Monitoring builds this self-belief by way of making AI behavior transparent and responsible.

Simple performance signs offer significant insights without developing more workload. Time stored is one of the most realistic signs. If AI workflows continuously reduce turnaround time, they are delivering real value. If time savings decrease, it can imply inefficiencies or growing complexity that desires attention. The quantity of revisions required is some other treasured signal. Frequent corrections advocate that AI instructions can be doubtful or that the workflow no longer suits modern-day necessities. Fewer revisions suggest solid and nicely-aligned approaches.

Consumer delight additionally performs a key position. Comments from teachers, analysts, developers, or directors well-known shows how AI influences day by day work. Even though outputs are technically accurate, frustration or confusion amongst users shows a want for development. Tracking also helps determine whilst retraining or refinement is necessary. AI does no longer automatically alter to new expectancies unless workflows are up to date. Normal assessment classes allow teams to refine activates, update templates, and enhance accuracy based totally on real usage rather than assumptions.

Importantly, tracking keeps AI aligned with organizational desires. AI needs to help outcomes such as performance, first-rate, and consistency. While tracking specializes in these desires, AI remains a strategic asset rather than a disconnected tool. Monitoring ought to be handled as a habitual interest, now not a corrective action. When built into regular paintings cycles, it will become an herbal a part of AI usage. Teams that screen continually are better geared up to scale AI accurately and confidently, ensuring that technology continues to serve human beings instead of complicates their work.

7.6 SCALING AI ACROSS TEAMS

Scaling AI across teams is a behavioral and organizational process rather than just a technical one. Many businesses erroneously believe that once AI is successful in one field, it should be used everywhere right away. Confusion, resistance, and uneven outcomes are common outcomes of this strategy. Patience, clarity, and a solid foundation based on reliable workflows are necessary for effective scalability. AI is most useful when it is integrated into routine tasks rather than being a stand-alone or experimental tool. Teams must concentrate on progressive growth, mutual understanding, and useful integration into current procedures in order to accomplish this. Only when users have faith in the system and feel comfortable utilizing it will scaling be successful.

Gradual Expansion through Stable Workflows

Stability should always be the first step in scaling. It is crucial to make sure that at least one workflow is operating dependably before implementing AI across several teams or departments. A stable workflow is one in which users are aware of their responsibilities, review procedures are transparent, and outputs are consistent. Scaling just makes pre-existing issues worse in the absence of this stability.

A structured approach to scaling AI across teams can be described through the following stages:

1. **Start with one clearly defined workflow**: the first step is to select an unmarried procedure that is repetitive, low-hazard, and properly understood. This will be report generation, documentation drafting, or data summarization. That specializes in one workflow permits groups to check AI in managed surroundings and discover gaps without overwhelming customers.
2. **Refine and stabilize the workflow:** as soon as AI is introduced, the workflow has to be delicate via repeated use. Prompts are adjusted, input codecs are standardized, and assessment checkpoints are brought. Stability is completed whilst outputs are predictable and require minimum correction. This degree builds accept as true with inside the device.
3. **Report the workflow definitely:** clean documentation plays a vital position in scaling. It explains what the AI does, what inputs it wishes, what outputs it produces, and wherein human evaluation is required. Documentation gets rid of uncertainty and ensures that new customers comply with the identical technique rather than experimenting randomly.
4. **Proportion first-class practices throughout groups:** as the workflow matures, instructions discovered have to be shared. This includes powerful prompts, common errors, and overview tips. Shared exceptional practices reduce the gaining knowledge of curve for brand spanking new teams and create consistency in how AI is used throughout the organization.

5. **Introduce AI to a 2d, similar workflow:** Scaling must circulate horizontally earlier than moving vertically. As opposed to automating absolutely different tactics, groups ought to apply AI to similar responsibilities in which the same good judgment may be reused. This minimizes hazard and accelerates adoption.
6. **Train groups gradually, now not all of sudden:** training has to be phased. Introducing AI to a small organization of customers first allows them to turn out to be comfy and assured. Those early adopters frequently emerge as internal champions who help others study and reduce resistance.
7. **Integrate AI into each day workouts:** AI must now not feel like a further step. Scaling is effective best whilst AI will become a part of current workflows consisting of weekly making plans, reporting cycles, or evaluation techniques. When AI is embedded into daily routines, adoption feels herbal as opposed to pressured.
8. **Screen usage and adjust constantly:** Scaling does no longer stop with deployment. Groups have to screen how AI is used, wherein it adds cost, and in which it causes friction. Ordinary comments enables refine workflows and guarantees that AI keeps to assist real wishes.

Gradual scaling reduces overload and prevents burnout. When people feel pushed to adopt too many tools at once, resistance increases. A measured approach allows teams to adapt at their own pace while maintaining quality and confidence. Clear documentation and shared practices act as anchors during scaling. They provide consistency and reduce dependence on individual knowledge. Over time, AI stops being seen as a separate system and becomes a normal part of how work gets done.

7.7 MAINTAINING LONG-TERM RELIABILITY

Long-term reliability in AI systems isn't always something that occurs automatically as soon as a workflow is installation. Many groups assume that once an AI method begins working successfully, it's going to hold to do so all the time. In fact, AI workflows exist in converting environments. Statistics codecs evolve, enterprise needs shift, and expectations from outputs steadily boom. Because of this, reliability depends less on the initial setup and more on how continuously the system is reviewed and guided over time. Without everyday attention, even a well-designed AI workflow can slowly lose accuracy and relevance. Human oversight performs a vital function in keeping reliability. AI systems operate based on the instructions, examples, and facts they receive. Whilst those inputs now not replicate modern-day realities, outputs start to glide.

Human reviewers help become aware of those subtle adjustments early. By way of checking effects periodically, teams can seize inaccuracies, previous language, or misaligned insights before they affect decisions or outside communication. This oversight does now not require steady tracking; however it does require planned and intentional evaluate cycles. Some other vital element is variation to changing facts. Over time, the nature of records flowing into AI workflows frequently adjustments. Survey questions may be updated, consumer conduct might also shift, or reporting requirements can also amplify. If AI workflows are not adjusted accordingly, they'll maintain processing information using outdated assumptions.

This can lead to misleading summaries or incomplete outcomes. Normal updates make sure that workflows stay aligned with modern-day records structures and organizational desires, preserving consider in AI-generated outputs. Spark off layout and templates additionally want periodic refinement. Activates that worked well within the early degrees may also come to be much less effective as expectations grow. Groups may additionally want extra unique insights, extraordinary codecs, or progressed tone in outputs. Reviewing and refining prompts permits AI structures to adapt along person needs. Small upgrades, implemented consistently, often result in noticeable gains in output best and reliability over the years. Reliability is also closely connected to consistency in assessment practices. When teams treat AI preservation as an occasional challenge, issues generally tend to accumulate.

In comparison, groups that construct ordinary take a look at-ins into their workflows keep better confidence in AI results. These check-ins help make sure that AI continues to aid work rather than introduce uncertainty. Consistency in interest creates stability, while gear and requirements alternate. Ultimately, long-time period reliability is not accomplished through one-time configuration or advanced technical features. Its miles constructed via ongoing care, considerate oversight, and a willingness to alter. AI works nice when its miles handled as a dynamic device in preference to a static tool. While groups take delivery of that reliability grows from non-stop engagement, AI turns into a reliable accomplice that offers value over the long run as opposed to a short-lived test.

7.8 SECURITY AND DATA HANDLING

The adoption of AI in normal workflows has brought new duties along its benefits. As AI structures increasingly cope with documents, survey responses, instructional records, technical files, and inner reports, organizations need to pay close attention to how facts is accessed, processed, and stored. Protection and records dealing with are not non-obligatory issues; they're crucial to constructing believe in AI-pushed operations. Without clean safeguards, even the greenest AI workflow can come to be a source of threat. AI structures regularly have interaction with touchy facts along with personal details, confidential commercial enterprise records, or institutional information. While this records flows through automated approaches, the capacity affect of misuse or exposure increases. For this reason, organizations should technique AI adoption with a clear understanding of the way data actions thru their systems and who has control over it.

Defining statistics access and usage boundaries

The foundation of comfortable AI usage lies in definitely defining what data an AI machine is authorized to procedure. Not all records within an enterprise have to be reachable to AI tools. A few statistics can be too sensitive, regulated, or inappropriate to the task at hand. Setting up obstacles guarantees that AI is used responsibly and best wherein it provides cost. Clear policies assist teams apprehend which datasets can be uploaded, analyzed, or shared within AI workflows. These rules should also specify who is legal to provoke AI procedures and assessment outputs. When get entry to be limited to specific roles, the hazard of unintended publicity or misuse is significantly decreased.

Controlled access also makes accountability simpler, as it turns into clean who is chargeable for managing AI-driven duties. Any other essential component of defining obstacles understands the purpose of statistics utilization. AI must process information most effective to acquire a particular, approved goal. the usage of records past its meant motive now not handiest increases danger but can also damage accept as true with amongst clients, students, or users. Purpose-pushed information managing keeps AI aligned with moral and operational requirements.

Secure Storage and Responsible Output Management

As soon as AI has processed information, the question of in which outputs are stored turns into vital. AI-generated summaries, reports, or analyses frequently contain the identical level of sensitivity as the original facts. Storing these outputs without right safeguards can divulge groups to pointless threat. Secure storage practices make certain that AI outputs are protected inside the same manner as other essential documents. Get entry to controls, internal repositories, and clear retention guidelines assist prevent unauthorized use. It is equally critical to determine how long AI-generated information must be saved and while it should be deleted. Maintaining information longer than vital will increase publicity without adding fee. Responsible output control additionally entails reviewing AI-generated content before it's far shared. Human oversight ensures that touchy info isn't unintentionally protected in reviews or communications.

This review step acts as a final safeguard, allowing organizations to maintain control over what statistics leaves their structures. Protection consciousness plays an important function in lengthy-time period AI adoption. When teams apprehend the significance of careful facts coping with, they're much more likely to follow hooked up practices continuously. This shared responsibility strengthens organizational self-belief in AI structures and encourages wider, safer usage. By prioritizing safety and statistics dealing with, organizations create a solid basis for AI-driven paintings. Accountable practices not best lessen threat but also construct trust amongst stakeholders, making AI a reliable and sustainable tool for normal operations.

7.9 BEST PRACTICES FOR SUSTAINABLE SCALING

Sustainable scaling of AI isn't about velocity or most automation. It is approximately balance. While businesses rush to automate the whole lot at once, they frequently lose manage, clarity, and agree with within the device. Proper sustainability comes from information in which automation provides price and where human judgment has to remain primary. AI must enhance performance without weakening accountability, context, or selection-making. When this balance is maintained, scaling will become solid as opposed to volatile. One of the most important principles of sustainable scaling is treating AI as an operating partner, no longer a substitute for human beings. AI performs exceptional while it supports humans through coping with repetitive, structured, and time-ingesting responsibilities. Human beings, on the other hand, deliver judgment, creativity, ethical reasoning, and contextual expertise.

While groups try to take away human beings absolutely from workflows, mistakes increase and confidence in AI outputs decreases. Sustainable systems absolutely outline what AI is chargeable for and where human evaluate or approval is needed. As AI usage expands, workflows should evolve based totally on actual enjoy rather than assumptions. What works properly in small tests might also want adjustment at scale. Hit groups actively accumulate feedback from customers who engage with AI structures day by day. This remark highlights gaps, misunderstandings, and areas where AI outputs may also experience widespread or misaligned with expectancies. As opposed to viewing those troubles as failures, mature groups treat them as mastering possibilities and refine workflows as a consequence. Some other critical element of sustainable scaling is adaptability.

AI systems are not static tools. Records modifications, enterprise wishes evolve, and person expectations shift over time. Workflows that are not reviewed frequently come to be outdated and unreliable. Organizations that scale AI successfully builds exercises for reviewing activates, templates, and outputs. Small refinements made always prevent large troubles later and make sure that AI remains relevant and beneficial. Accept as true with performs a vital position in long-term AI adoption. Groups will simplest rely upon AI structures in the event that they apprehend how outcomes are produced and sense assured in their accuracy. Transparency in workflows builds this trust.

When humans understand in which AI is used, what inputs it gets, and the way outputs are reviewed, resistance decreases? Clean communication about AI's function prevents worry and incorrect information and encourages accountable use. Sustainable scaling also relies upon on sensible expectations. AI is powerful, but it isn't always perfect. Expecting ideal output results in unhappiness and misuse. Organizations that scale responsibly take delivery of that AI will make mistakes and layout systems that detect and correct them early. This attitude reduces risk and helps steady increase as opposed to unexpected breakdowns. Whilst these practices are followed, AI shifts from being a brief productiveness improve to an extended-term organizational asset. It becomes a part of ordinary work, quietly enhancing efficiency at the same time as ultimate underneath human control. Responsible scaling ensures that AI grows with the company rather than outpacing it, developing systems which are reliable, adaptable, and trusted over time.

A. SHORT QUESTIONS

1. What is meant by optimization in AI workflows?
2. Why do AI workflows sometimes produce inconsistent results?
3. What are common issues faced during AI implementation?
4. How does prompt refinement improve AI output quality?
5. Why is human review important in AI-driven workflows?
6. What is meant by troubleshooting in AI systems?
7. How does monitoring help improve AI performance?
8. Why should AI workflows be scaled gradually?
9. What role does data quality play in AI optimization?
10. How does long-term maintenance support reliable AI usage?

B. LONG QUESTIONS

1. Explain the need for optimization after implementing AI workflows.
2. Discuss common problems encountered in AI workflows and their solutions.

3. Explain the importance of prompt refinement and structured inputs in improving AI accuracy.
4. Describe how organizations can scale AI workflows safely and responsibly.
5. Analyze the role of monitoring, review, and maintenance in sustaining AI systems over time.

C. MULTIPLE CHOICE QUESTIONS (MCQS)

1. Optimization of AI workflows mainly focuses on:

   a) Increasing automation speed only
   b) Improving accuracy and consistency
   c) Eliminating human involvement
   d) Increasing system complexity

2. One major cause of AI errors is:

   a) Too much monitoring **b)** Poor data quality
   c) Clear instructions **d)** Regular review

3. Prompt refinement helps in:

   a) Reducing clarity **b)** Making outputs more consistent
   c) Increasing randomness **d)** Avoiding AI usage

4. Human review in AI workflows is important to:

   a) Delay processes **b)** Increase workload
   c) Validate and control outputs **d)** Replace automation

5. Troubleshooting in AI systems involves:

   a) Ignoring errors **b)** Identifying and correcting issues
   c) Removing AI tools **d)** Avoiding workflows

6. Monitoring AI performance helps organizations to:

   a) Stop automation **b)** Track efficiency and accuracy
   c) Increase risks **d)** Eliminate reporting

7. Scaling AI workflows should be:

   a) Immediate and complete **b)** Random and experimental
   c) Gradual and controlled **d)** Avoided

8. Which factor is essential for long-term AI reliability?

a) One-time setup
b) Continuous review and improvement
c) No human involvement
d) Maximum automation

9. Data quality affects AI performance by:

a) Having no impact
b) Directly influencing output accuracy
c) Only slowing processes
d) Reducing automation

10. Sustainable AI scaling focuses on:

a) Speed over accuracy
b) Automation without control
c) Balance between AI and human judgment
d) Eliminating decision-making

CHAPTER 8

YOUR FIRST 90-DAY AI TRANSFORMATION

8.1 STARTING SMALL AND BUILDING CONFIDENCE

Adopting synthetic intelligence in a corporation is not most effective a technical selection but additionally a human one. Many AI initiatives fail no longer due to the fact the tools are ineffective, but because people experience uncertain, crushed, or proof against change. The muse of a hit AI adoption lies in mindset. When AI is approached as a supportive assistant rather than a chance, groups end up extra open to experimenting with it of their day by day paintings. Beginning small allows companies to explore AI's abilities without worry and construct self-assurance steadily via real revel in.

Seeing AI as a Helper, no longer a hazard

One of the most important obstacles to AI adoption is worry. Employees frequently worry that AI will update their roles or complicate existing processes. This worry increases whilst AI is added abruptly or on a big scale. To avoid this, corporations ought to body AI as a helper designed to lessen workload, no longer as an alternative for human attempt. While groups remember the fact that AI exists to handle repetitive and time-ingesting tasks, their notion starts off evolved to change. AI turns into a tool that frees them from recurring paintings as opposed to a machine those video display units or judges their overall performance. This shift in angle is critical for reputation.

Humans are greater inclined to interact with AI once they experience it supports their position and complements their effectiveness in preference to threatening their function. Treating AI as a helper additionally encourages curiosity. Crew contributors come to be extra open to trying small duties and watching outcomes. This creates a secure studying environment where experimentation is welcomed and errors are seen as part of the procedure. Confidence starts to develop obviously while humans recognize that AI can simplify paintings instead of complicate it.

Building Trust through Small and Practical Wins

Confidence in AI does no longer broaden thru demonstrations or promises alone. It grows thru practical achievement. The simplest manner to build agrees with is first of all responsibilities which are easy, repetitive, and low-threat. Those responsibilities allow groups to look immediately blessings without widespread consequences if something is going incorrect.

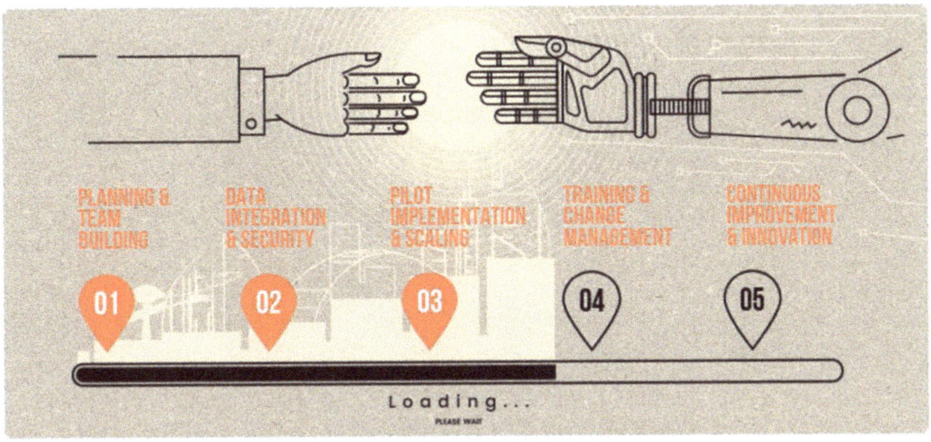

Figure 8.1: Starting AI adoption.

When AI efficiently completes small tasks, inclusive of drafting routine documents or organizing records, people begin to notice the time stored and attempt decreased. These early wins are effective because they're tangible. In preference to abstract benefits, teams enjoy real upgrades in their day by day work. As a result, resistance starts to vanish naturally. Consistency plays an important function in building self-belief. When AI supplies dependable results time and again, trust strengthens through the years. Teams emerge as extra relaxed relying on AI and start to discover additional use cases. This gradual growth feels secure due to the fact it's far primarily based on proven experience in place of assumptions. Starting small also permits businesses to refine their method.

Groups can regulate commands, overview strategies, and expectancies before scaling AI in addition. This gaining knowledge of phase prevents frustration and helps build a stable foundation for lengthy-term adoption. Self-assurance built through small successes guarantees that AI adoption is sustainable and welcomed rather than compelled. Through starting with potential steps and specializing in agree with, groups create an environment where AI is conventional as an herbal a part of everyday work. This self-belief becomes the using force at the back of a hit and lasting AI transformation.

8.2 THE FIRST 30 DAYS: FOUNDATIN PHASE

The first thirty days of AI adoption are crucial because they have a lasting impact on how teams view and utilize AI. Large-scale automation or speed is not the focus of this phase.

It is about creating comfort, understanding, and reasonable expectations. Many businesses erroneously push AI too hard at first, which frequently results in misunderstandings or disappointment. By concentrating on preparation, experimentation, and learning from actual data, the foundation phase avoids this.

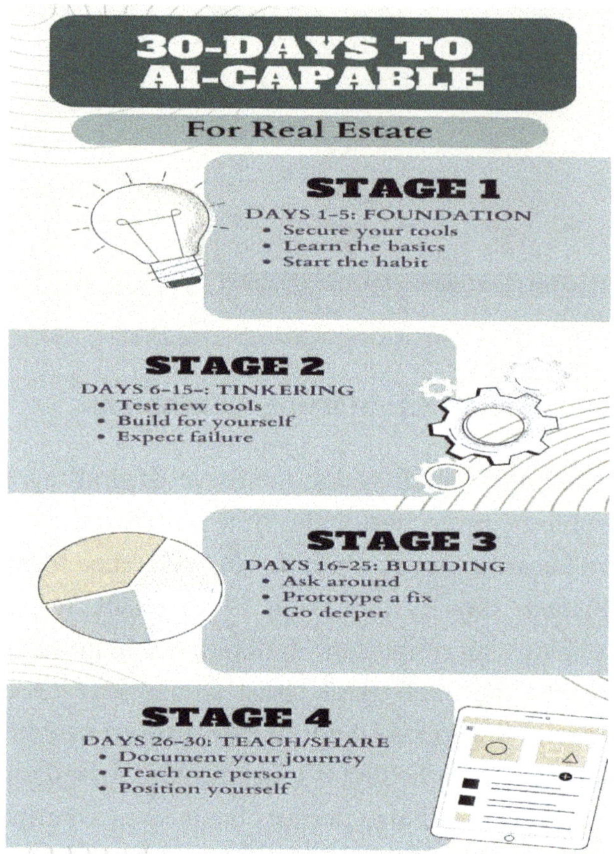

Figure 8.2: AI foundation phase.

AI should be implemented this month as a supplementary tool rather than to replace current procedures. Teams need time to see how AI acts, where it works well, and where human judgment is still needed. Perfection is not the goal; familiarity is. Users should be comfortable dealing with AI and evaluating its results by the conclusion of this phase.

Key Activities during the First 30 Days

1. **Identifying one repetitive task**: the inspiration phase ought to start with project choice. Rather of selecting a complicated or important manner, groups should perceive one simple and repetitive challenge that consumes time regularly. This

will be drafting habitual files, summarizing feedback, organizing information, or preparing trendy reviews. Selecting a low-risk mission reduces strain and permits teams to consciousness on studying instead of demanding about mistakes. A clear undertaking additionally enables outline success, making it easier to evaluate whether or not AI is absolutely including value.

2. **Choosing suitable AI tools:** once the mission is diagnosed, the next step is selecting the proper AI device for the activity. No longer all AI gear serves the identical motive, and the usage of the wrong tool can create needless complexity. At some point of this section, groups need to prioritize ease of use over superior capabilities. Gear with simple interfaces and clean outputs are ideal for novices. The purpose is not to master every function however to understand how AI suits into present workflows without disrupting them.
3. **Growing easy prompts or templates:** AI plays nice while it receives clean commands. Within the foundation segment, activates and templates ought to be saved simple and direct. Overly complicated instructions can confuse new customers and lead to inconsistent results. Developing fundamental prompts allows teams apprehend how AI responds to different inputs and how small adjustments affect output fine. Templates additionally introduce consistency, making it less complicated to examine outcomes across multiple attempts and learn from them.
4. **Trying out outputs on small samples:** Experimentation is the center of the first thirty days. In place of the use of big datasets or complete workloads, teams must test AI on small samples. This reduces hazard and makes it less difficult to review effects cautiously. Checking out permits users to spot errors, apprehend obstacles, and adjust expectancies. It also encourages discussion within the group about what works well and what wishes development. These small exams offer treasured insights that manual future enlargement.

By focusing on these activities, the foundation phase creates a safe environment for learning. Teams gain hands-on experience without pressure, and AI becomes familiar rather than intimidating. At the end of the first thirty days, workflows may not be perfect, but that is not the goal. Success at this stage means that teams feel comfortable using AI as a support system and are ready to move toward deeper automation with confidence.

8.3 THE SECOND 30 DAYS: AUTOMATION PHASE

Teams go into a phase where confidence starts to convert into action after the initial learning phase. Moving from standalone AI usage to linked workflows that manage actual work is the focus of the second thirty days. Organizations are now aware of the capabilities of AI, and confidence has begun to grow. Automation that results in quantifiable time savings and lessens repeated effort is now the main focus.

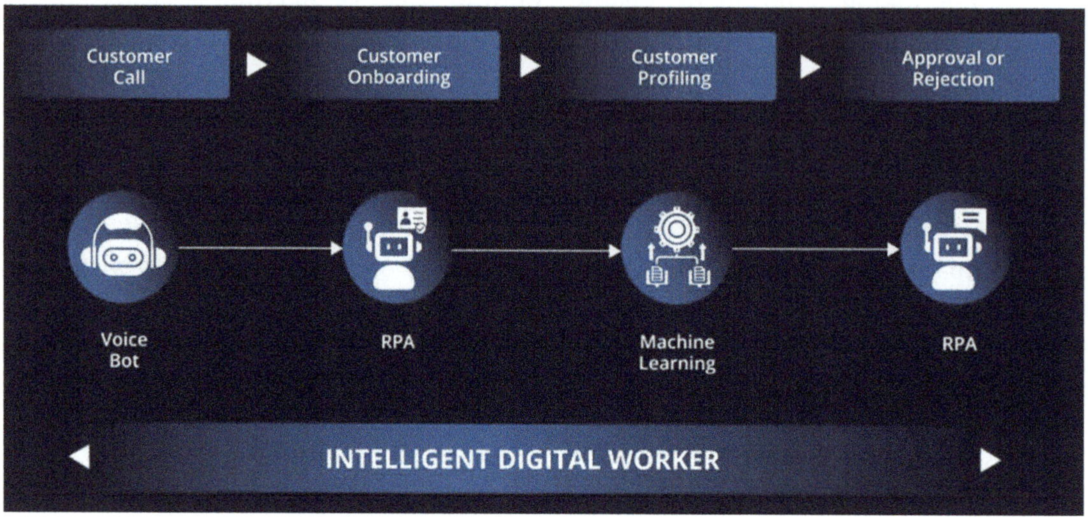

Figure 8.3: AI automation phase.

Source: *(Akash Takyar, 2025)*

This stage is crucial because it transforms AI from a useful assistant into a trustworthy operational partner. Teams start connecting jobs so that work flows seamlessly from beginning to end rather than employing AI for individual tasks. The goal is to reliably automate one entire workflow rather than to automate everything at once.

Building a Complete and Reliable Workflow

Organizations should focus on one weekly time-consuming recurrent process throughout the automation phase. Survey analysis, lesson planning, report writing, and documentation updates are a few examples of this. Choosing a predictable and well-understood workflow is crucial.

The automation process during this phase typically involves the following steps:

1. **Automating one complete workflow**: the first priority is to choose a single workflow and automate it cease to end. This means figuring out where the project starts off evolved, how information actions between steps, and what the final output looks as if. While AI handles the complete collection as opposed to man or woman

moves, the time savings become in reality visible. Teams no longer switch among gear or repeat the same steps manually, which improves efficiency and recognition.

2. **Including review checkpoints for control:** Automation does no longer imply eliminating human oversight. Evaluate checkpoints are important to make certain accuracy and accountability. These checkpoints allow people to validate AI-generated outputs earlier than they're shared with customers, students, or stakeholders. Via placing assessment degrees at key points, companies hold believes at the same time as profiting from automation. This stability reassures groups that quality remains below control.
3. **Standardizing output formats:** Consistency turns into vital as automation will increase. In the course of this section, teams should standardize formats for reports, documents, summaries, or communications generated by means of AI. Fashionable formats reduce confusion, speed up reviews, and create a professional appearance. When outputs observe the equal structure on every occasion, groups spend much less attempt correcting format and greater time improving content material.
4. **Reducing manual repetition throughout responsibilities:** one of the fundamental goals of this section is to dispose of repeated guide moves. Tasks which include copying facts, rewriting similar content material, or reorganizing records need to be handled through AI wherever possible. As repetition decreases, human effort shifts toward reviewing insights, making selections, and adding contextual know-how. This transformation significantly improves productivity and process satisfaction.

AI starts to handle a discernible amount of routine labor as these techniques are put into practice. Instead of weeks, the difference is frequently noticeable in a matter of days. Teams have more predictable timetables, less workload pressure, and fewer delays. AI should stop feeling experimental by the conclusion of the second thirty days. It discreetly supports processes in the background as it becomes a part of the regular workflow. While AI oversees implementation, humans are still in charge of judgment and guidance. This stage lays the groundwork for scale and optimization in the transformation's last phase.

8.4 THE FINAL 30 DAYS: OPTIMIZATION AND SCALING PHASE

A critical shift occurs in the last thirty days of an AI adoption journey. This stage is no longer about learning the fundamentals or experimenting. The goal is to make AI a dependable, consistent, and trustworthy component of daily tasks. Teams have actually connected AI to actual workflows and tested it on modest jobs by this point. The emphasis now is on regulated expansion, stability, and refinement.

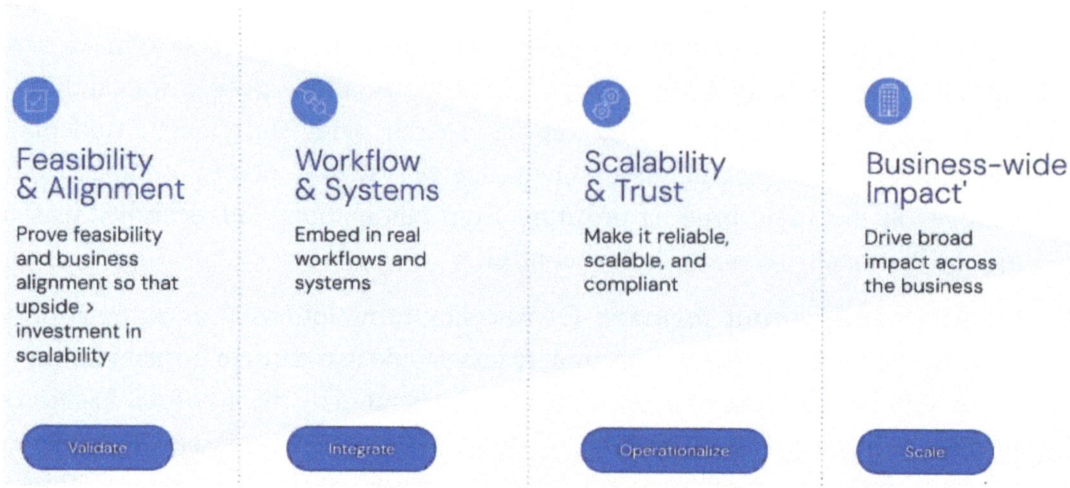

Figure 8.4: Optimization and scaling phase.

During this time, businesses start concentrating on how well AI functions rather than whether it works at all. Excitement gives way to discipline. Whether AI stays a short-term experiment or develops into a long-term operational asset depends on small, steady gains made throughout this phase.

Refining, Expanding, and Stabilizing AI Workflows

Optimization is the main goal of the last thirty days. Teams thoroughly review current AI procedures to find holes, inefficiencies, and problems with quality. This review aids in turning acceptable results into reliable ones. Teams enhance current systems rather than implementing completely new ones.

Key activities during this phase include the following:

- **Reviewing workflow performance**: teams examine how AI workflows have done over the last weeks. They have a look at wherein outputs had been correct, in which human intervention was required, and in which delays came about. This evaluate isn't about blaming gear or human beings, but about expertise actual utilization styles. By analyzing real performance, groups benefit readability on which parts of the workflow are robust and which want adjustment. This insight lets in for targeted upgrades in place of pointless changes.

- **Enhancing consistency and output quality:** Consistency becomes a concern on this section. AI outputs have to follow the same structure, tone, and standards on every occasion they are generated. Groups refine activates, templates, and commands to reduce variation. Small adjustments, inclusive of clearer formatting policies or more particular commands, considerably improve reliability. As consistency improves, consider in AI evidently will increase throughout the employer.
- **Expanding AI utilization to comparable duties:** once a workflow proves stable, teams can observe the same common sense to associated tasks. As an example, if AI effectively generates one type of report, it can be tailored to generate similar reviews with minimal attempt. This growth feels safe as it builds on verified success instead of experimentation. Controlled growth helps companies advantage more value from AI without overwhelming customers or systems.
- **Documenting first-rate practices and learnings:** Documentation will become critical at some point of this section. Teams file what labored, what failed, and how troubles were resolved. These nice practices function inner guidance for modern-day and destiny customers. Clean documentation guarantees that AI usage does now not depend upon an unmarried person's knowledge. It additionally makes onboarding less complicated and prevents repeated mistakes.

AI gradually becomes part of everyday life as optimization progresses. Team members begin to see it as an integral part of regular operations rather than as a distinct tool. AI-assisted workflows now automatically route requests that were previously handled manually. This change reflects adoption maturity. AI is no longer being tested by the conclusion of the last thirty days. It develops into a dependable mechanism that silently supports work. Teams are more confident because AI is reliable, effective, and in line with actual needs rather than because it is novel. This stage guarantees the long-term sustainability of AI adoption in addition to its success.

8.5 WEEKLY MILESTONES AND ACCOUNTABILITY

Lengthy-term transformation frequently fails not due to the fact goals are uncertain, however because development feels remote and overwhelming. When groups try to trade their working fashion over a ninety-day period, the timeline can seem too lengthy to maintain cognizance and motivation. Breaking this era into weekly milestones creates an experience of course and keeps teams engaged in the course of the adventure. Weekly goals transform an abstract plan into a series of plausible moves that feel realistic and inside attain. Quick-time period milestones make development visible. While teams can see what has been finished within an unmarried week, self-belief increases clearly.

Instead of ready months to evaluate fulfillment, small wins are identified often. This steady reinforcement encourages endured participation and decreases resistance to change. Weekly shape also affords readability, ensuring that everyone is familiar with what desires to be done and whilst it wishes to show up. A weekly technique brings rhythm to implementation. Groups start to increase a dependancy of reviewing, adjusting, and enhancing their use of AI. This rhythm prevents lengthy gaps among moves, which frequently lead to confusion or loss of hobby. With clean weekly expectancies, individuals stay aligned and targeted on regular improvement in preference to dashing closer to unrealistic effects.

Constructing responsibility via regular take a look at-Ins

Responsibility plays a crucial function in sustained adoption. Without everyday take a look at-ins, small troubles can pass unnoticed and step by step grow into large issues. Weekly reviews create space for reflection and dialogue, permitting groups to become aware of challenges early and correct path before momentum is lost. That test-ins isn't approximately criticism however about studying and development.

Everyday accountability encourages responsibility at both character and crew ranges. Whilst progress is reviewed weekly, people are more likely to follow thru on commitments. This feel of duty enables prevent delays and guarantees that adoption moves ahead progressively. Duty additionally fosters transparency, as crew contributors sense comfy sharing what is working and what wishes adjustment.

Weekly take a look at-ins aid realistic pacing. In place of pushing for fast transformation, teams attention on regular, sustainable progress. This reduces strain and stops burnout. Consistency turns into the priority, allowing AI workflows to adapt obviously through exercise and comments. Through the years, this technique builds self-belief and competence, making AI an included part of day by day paintings rather than a pressured initiative.

Through emphasizing weekly milestones and duty, groups create surroundings wherein progress is non-stop and workable. Small, constant moves compound into meaningful transformation. This disciplined approach guarantees that adoption remains consistent, targeted, and aligned with long-time period desires, proving that consistency sincerely matters greater than pace.

8.6 MEASURING RESULTY AND RETURN ON EFFORT

Synthetic intelligence adoption frequently generates excitement, but exhilaration on my own does now not guarantee price. Many groups test with AI tools without clearly knowledge whether or not the ones gear are virtually enhancing paintings results. Measuring results and go back on attempt is critical to ensure that AI is handing over realistic benefits rather than simply appearing innovative. The actual achievement of AI lies not in how advanced it seems, however in how efficiently it improves every day work. Whilst companies focus on measurable results, AI adoption will become greater intentional and sustainable. Clear size helps teams apprehend what is working, what desires development, and in which similarly funding makes feel.

Comparing sensible impact in normal work

The maximum significant manner to evaluate AI is by using watching the way it affects ordinary responsibilities. Practical indicators including time stored, discount in guide errors, and stepped forward consistency provide a practical photo of AI's impact. These signs are smooth to observe and directly connected to each day operations. Time savings are regularly the first visible gain. While AI reduces the time required to research records, draft documents, or put together reviews, teams at once feel the distinction. Even saving a small quantity of time on a repeated undertaking can accumulate into sizable profits over weeks and months. This reclaimed time lets in employees to focus on higher-price sports along with decision-making, creativity, and client interplay.

Errors reduction is some other crucial measure. Manual paintings, particularly when repetitive, are liable to mistakes caused by fatigue or oversight. AI helps standardize strategies and practice the identical guidelines constantly. Fewer mistakes cause better pleasant outputs and decrease the want for remodel, which in addition saves time and assets. Consistency is equally essential, mainly for businesses that supply reviews, instructions, or technical outputs regularly. AI ensures that comparable tasks are dealt with inside the same manner every time. This consistency improves reliability and builds consider amongst stakeholders, customers, and internal groups.

Using Simple Metrics to Build Long-Term Value

Measuring AI overall performance does now not require complex structures or advanced analytics. Simple metrics are frequently more effective because they're simpler to music and recognize. Groups can evaluate how lengthy a task took before AI adoption versus after implementation, or how many revisions had been needed previously compared to now. These straightforward comparisons offer clean evidence of development. Small upgrades may additionally seem insignificant in the beginning, but their effect grows thru repetition. A technique that saves fifteen mins every day might not seem dramatic, however over several months it translates into many hours of stored effort. While those enhancements arise across a couple of workflows, the cumulative value turns into considerable. Normal dimension also supports non-stop improvement. By means of reviewing consequences weekly or monthly, groups can discover styles and modify workflows consequently.

If AI outputs require common correction, prompts or templates may be subtle. If sure obligations show strong gains, similar tactics can be computerized subsequent. This cycle of size and refinement ensures that AI adoption evolves in a controlled and useful manner. Any other vital benefit of measuring effects is justification for future funding. Clear proof of time financial savings, pleasant development, and performance gains helps selection-makers expectantly spend money on higher tools, education, or expanded workflows. Instead of relying on assumptions or trends, corporations can base selections on tested effects. While AI adoption is guided through practical size, it turns into a strategic asset rather than an experimental device. Groups gain readability, self-belief, and route, making sure that AI contributes real cost to everyday paintings and lengthy-term organizational boom.

8.7 TRAINING AND TEAM ADOPTION

A hit AI transformation isn't always driven by technology alone. It relies upon in large part on how humans recognize, be given, and use AI in their each day paintings. Even the maximum advanced AI gear fails to supply cost if groups sense confused, intimidated, or immune to trade. For that reason, schooling must be slow and supportive in preference to rushed or imposed. Introducing AI slowly allows group participants to construct confidence over time. While human beings are given space to explore tools at their very own pace, they may be more likely to develop interest as opposed to worry.

Early schooling need to attention on simple, low-risk responsibilities that show clean benefits. As group contributors revel in small successes, their believe in AI grows obviously. This technique prevents overwhelm and decreases the tension frequently associated with new era. Encouraging experimentation is equally critical. Groups should feel safe trying AI equipment without worrying about making mistakes. While errors are treated as learning opportunities in place of disasters, people emerge as more open to innovation. This mindset creates a lifestyle wherein AI is visible as a beneficial assistant instead of a disruptive force.

Developing aid structures for long-term Adoption

Education by me is not enough to make certain long-time period AI adoption. Ongoing help structures play a vital role in supporting teams use AI continuously and successfully. Clean hints help customers recognize where AI fits into their workflow and wherein human judgment remains required. When expectations are surely defined, confusion and misuse are minimized. Shared templates and examples further boost up getting to know. In place of asking every team member to figure things out independently, corporations can provide prepared-made formats and sample workflows. Those resources act as reference points and decrease the trial-and-mistakes phase. Through the years, teams can refine and adapt those templates to fit their precise wishes, making AI usage more aligned with real work situations. Management aid is any other critical issue. Whilst managers and crew leads actively use AI and proportion their reviews, it sends a strong signal that AI is part of normal work practices.

This seen assist builds self-assurance among crew contributors and encourages wider participation. Adoption will become natural when human beings see practical blessings verified with the aid of their friends. Most significantly, teams have to recognize the position of AI inside the business enterprise. AI must not be perceived as a replacement for human understanding, but as a tool that complements efficiency and consistency. When humans clearly understand what AI is chargeable for and what remains below human manage, collaboration turns into smoother. This readability reduces resistance and builds agree with. While schooling is sluggish, support is non-stop, and expectations are clean, AI adoption turns into an herbal progression in preference to a forced initiative. groups that sense supported are extra willing to engage, research, and innovate, allowing AI to grow to be a meaningful part of everyday work.

8.8 AVOIDING COMMON ADOPTION MISTAKES

Many organizations warfare with AI adoption no longer due to the fact the technology lacks functionality, but due to the fact expectancies are set too high at the start. AI is frequently delivered with the hope that it will right away automate most tasks and dispose of guide attempt. When this does not appear speedy, sadness follows. The hassle is hardly ever the device itself; it's far the approach taken all through adoption. Unrealistic expectations create stress, confusion, and resistance amongst teams, which ultimately slows progress in preference to accelerating it. One of the maximum commonplace mistakes companies make is attempting to automate the entirety right now. In the excitement round AI, groups regularly try to observe it across multiple workflows simultaneously.

This overwhelms each the technology and the humans the usage of it. Instead of gaining clarity, customers come upon inconsistent outputs, doubtful approaches, and a loss of agree with in outcomes. AI works nice while delivered progressively. Starting with an unmarried, nicely-described challenge lets in teams to apprehend how the device behaves, how a lot assessment is needed, and where upgrades are required. Some other common difficulty is skipping evaluate steps. Some agencies expect that AI-generated outputs are continually correct and equipped for use. This assumption leads to mistakes being passed alongside without verification. AI structures function based on styles in information and instructions given to them. If inputs are unclear or data satisfactory is poor, outputs will mirror those weaknesses. Human review is not a transient requirement but an everlasting part of accountable AI utilization.

Overview degrees make certain accuracy, relevance, and alignment with organizational desires. Ignoring facts pleasant is some other predominant obstacle to a success adoption. AI is based closely at the statistics it processes. If the statistics is incomplete, old, or inconsistent, results can be unreliable. Many teams focus on improving activates and tools even as overlooking the quality of their input records. This leads to frustration whilst AI outputs do now not meet expectations. Ensuring easy, established, and applicable facts before automation substantially improves outcomes and reduces transform. Over-trusting AI is similarly unstable. Whilst AI can take care of repetitive duties efficaciously, it lacks context, judgment, and moral cognizance. Choices that require interpretation, emotional understanding, or strategic wondering need to usually involve humans.

Businesses that treat AI as an independent decision-maker often face problems related to accountability and credibility. AI should guide human decision-making, not update it completely. Persistence performs an essential position in a hit AI adoption. AI structures enhance through the years through refinement, remarks, and repeated use. Expecting ideal consequences within the early ranges sets teams up for disappointment. A disciplined approach that includes checking out, refining activates, monitoring outputs, and adjusting workflows ends in consistent improvement. Small gains accumulated over time produce significant transformation. A hit corporation's deal with AI adoption as an extended-term procedure instead of a short restores. They consciousness on constructing self-assurance, keeping manipulate, and studying from mistakes. by means of warding off rushed automation, respecting evaluate techniques, keeping records fine, and preserving human beings within the loop, organizations create a strong basis for AI to deliver actual price. Patience and field do no longer sluggish development; they make certain that progress lasts.

8.9 SUSTAINING AI IN DAILY WORK

Short-term testing or one-time implementation is not the paths to long-term success with artificial intelligence. It relies on how regularly AI is applied, evaluated, and refined over time. Businesses are more likely to experience long-term gains if they view AI as a tool for ongoing improvement rather than a permanent remedy. Successful teams incorporate AI into daily tasks until it becomes a natural part of how work is done, rather than seeing it as a complicated technology that needs ongoing attention. AI systems function in dynamic situations. Education priorities change, business demands change, and technology advances. Because of this, if workflows are not evaluated and modified, they may become less successful in the future. Instead than becoming antiquated or ineffective, continuous improvement guarantees that AI stays in line with actual needs. When businesses embrace this perspective, AI fosters expansion rather than stiffness.

Making AI Part of Everyday Work

When AI is smoothly integrated into day-to-day operations, its full potential becomes apparent. AI no longer seems like a stand-alone tool or an experimental feature at this point. It develops into a dependable support system that facilitates the accomplishment of regular chores, information organization, and regularity. With AI working in the background, workers begin to think about "doing work" rather than "using AI." This change occurs gradually. Teams may be careful at first, reviewing each output and using AI only for minor tasks. AI is eventually trusted with additional duties as confidence increases. Frequent use increases familiarity, which lowers resistance. Adoption of AI feels organic rather than forced when it is used on a regular basis. Sustainability requires ongoing evaluation and improvement. Teams can determine what is effective and what requires improvement through regular evaluation.

Accuracy and efficiency can be greatly increased by making minor changes to workflows, instructions, or review procedures. These improvements assist preserve confidence in AI-generated outputs by preventing small faults from developing into long-term ones. Adaptability is another crucial component of sustainability. Workflows for AI should be adaptable enough to alter as needs change. Existing workflows can be adjusted rather than replaced as new tasks arise or priorities change. This flexibility guarantees that AI will continue to support real work rather than restrict it, minimizing disruption. In the end, automation is not the only factor in long-term AI success. It is about developing habits of careful application, frequent assessment, and ongoing development. AI becomes a reliable component of everyday work when it is viewed as a developing collaborator rather than a fixed answer. Organizations can maintain productivity improvements and reap long-term benefits from AI without constantly reinventing thanks to this methodical, consistent approach.

Figure 8.5: Sustaining AI usage.

A. SHORT ANSWER QUESTIONS

1. What is meant by optimization in AI workflows?
2. Why do AI workflows sometimes produce inconsistent results?
3. What are common issues faced during AI implementation?
4. How does prompt refinement improve AI output quality?
5. Why is human review important in AI-driven workflows?
6. What is meant by troubleshooting in AI systems?
7. How does monitoring help improve AI performance?
8. Why should AI workflows be scaled gradually?
9. What role does data quality play in AI optimization?
10. How does long-term maintenance support reliable AI usage?

B. LONG QUESTIONS

1. Explain the need for optimization after implementing AI workflows.
2. Discuss common problems encountered in AI workflows and their solutions.

3. Explain the importance of prompt refinement and structured inputs in improving AI accuracy.
4. Describe how organizations can scale AI workflows safely and responsibly.
5. Analyze the role of monitoring, review, and maintenance in sustaining AI systems over time.

C. MULTIPLE CHOICE QUESTIONS (MCQS)

1. Optimization of AI workflows mainly focuses on:

   a) Increasing automation speed only

   b) Improving accuracy and consistency

   c) Eliminating human involvement

   d) Increasing system complexity

2. One major cause of AI errors is:

   a) Too much monitoring

   b) Poor data quality

   c) Clear instructions

   d) Regular review

3. Prompt refinement helps in:

   a) Reducing clarity

   b) Making outputs more consistent

   c) Increasing randomness

   d) Avoiding AI usage

4. Human review in AI workflows is important to:

   a) Delay processes

b) Increase workload

c) Validate and control outputs

d) Replace automation

5. Troubleshooting in AI systems involves:

   a) Ignoring errors

   b) Identifying and correcting issues

   c) Removing AI tools

   d) Avoiding workflows

6. Monitoring AI performance helps organizations to:

   a) Stop automation

   b) Track efficiency and accuracy

   c) Increase risks

   d) Eliminate reporting

7. Scaling AI workflows should be:

   a) Immediate and complete

   b) Random and experimental

   c) Gradual and controlled

   d) Avoided

8. Which factor is essential for long-term AI reliability?

   a) One-time setup

   b) Continuous review and improvement

c) No human involvement

d) Maximum automation

9. Data quality affects AI performance by:

a) Having no impact

b) Directly influencing output accuracy

c) Only slowing processes

d) Reducing automation

10. Sustainable AI scaling focuses on:

a) Speed over accuracy

b) Automation without control

c) Balance between AI and human judgment

d) Eliminating decision-making

www.ingramcontent.com/pod-product-compliance
Ingram Content Group UK Ltd.
Pitfield, Milton Keynes, MK11 3LW, UK
UKHW061539190726
13845UKWH00031B/1126

9 789347 006623